Drops into an Ocean

This book is dedicated with love and respect to
Peter Parkinson and Esther Smith
co-founders of Caring For Life

Drops into an Ocean

Juliet Barker

CANTERBURY
PRESS

© Caring For Life and Juliet Barker, 2017

First published in 2017 by Canterbury Press
Editorial office
3rd Floor, Invicta House,
108–114 Golden Lane,
London EC1Y 0TG.

Ancient
&Modern

Hymns Ancient & Modern® is a registered trademark of
Hymns Ancient and Modern Ltd.

Canterbury Press is an imprint of Hymns Ancient & Modern
Ltd (a registered charity)
13A Hellesdon Park Road, Norwich,
Norfolk, NR6 5DR, UK

www.canterburypress.co.uk

British Library Cataloguing in Publication data

A catalogue record for this book is available
from the British Library

978 1-78622-014-1

Printed and bound in Great Britain by
CPI Group (UK) Ltd

Caring For Life's 30th Birthday Song

We bring our broken world to You,
The One who sees each tear
You see the hurt, the shame and pain
You understand each fear.

We bring ourselves, for how can we
Begin to meet this need?
Rebuilding lives, not only homes;
Not only mouths to feed.

Chorus
We bring our loaves and fishes
To You, the Lord of all.
We'll follow in Your footsteps,
And answer to Your call.

Lord, take our small resources,
Take every loving deed.
Turn drops into an ocean
To meet a world of need.

We'll share Your love, Lord Jesus Christ,
In everything we do.
In caring for this broken world
We'll try to be like You.

Chorus

To You be all the glory, Lord
For every rescued soul;
For every person found a home,
And every life made whole.

Chorus

Turn drops into an ocean
To meet a world of need.

Contents

Foreword

I have visited Crag House Farm under many guises during the last 13 years, in a formal capacity as Lord-Lieutenant of West Yorkshire and, more important, to escort the charity's patron, HRH The Countess of Wessex, who is dedicated to the aims of Caring For Life and confers regularly with the executive committee on the charity's future.

Informally, I have relished the Christmas celebrations many times, have attended the summer Open Day which brings supporters over vast distances to come together, to pray and to celebrate. I have been delighted to see tricky passages from Shakespeare delivered impressively by young people supported by Caring For Life and there have been many concerts given by very well-rehearsed beneficiaries which have given joy to my husband and me. We have even driven a horse and carriage at the farm, following the Countess's lead.

From personal experience I know how all-encompassing the love given by the Parkinsons and Esther is. I was a bit low physically last winter. When Peter heard about it, he and Jonathan drove over to our village near York, just for coffee, to bring me gifts and to make sure all was well. It was hugely generous, both in terms of time and energy, and typical of their unstinted giving. The visit was followed up by a wonderfully happy lunch in the Granary with all the family present and a hamper of further gifts from them all.

Giving is central to Caring For Life. Everyone privileged to come under its wing at Crag House Farm or as a recipient of regular outreach visits has been given such love, hope and faith, that their difficult lives have been transformed. It is the finest example I know of Christian love in action.

Dame Ingrid Roscoe
Lord-Lieutenant of West Yorkshire

1

Learning from the Best

It is never easy to put yourself in someone else's place, particularly when that person's life is a world away from your own. For those of us who are blessed with a loving family, good friends and more than we need to live on, it can be particularly hard. How can we relate to the people we see sleeping rough on the streets of our cities? The drunks and drug-addicts lying in a stupor in doorways or staggering past shouting abuse at passers-by? The unemployed spending their days watching television, smoking cannabis or popping pills, and living off benefits instead of actively seeking work? The selfish and feckless, happy to have casual sex but not to provide for the unfortunate children they create?

Our disapproval is stirred up to outrage when we see such people on *The Jeremy Kyle Show* and *Benefits Britain*, or read tabloid headlines exposing the 'staggering scale of Britain's underclass' and screaming that 'half a million problem families cost the taxpayer £30 BILLION a year'.[1] Why should we, who take our personal responsibilities seriously, working long hours so that we can look after our dependants and pay our taxes, have to pick up the pieces for those who cannot be bothered to do it for themselves? And, more importantly, why should our hard-earned money be 'raked in' by 'lazy bums' who would rather live on state 'handouts' than find an honest job and whose ultimate nightmare is that 'When the telly goes off ... I don't know what we're going to do'?[2]

---

[1] www.dailymail.co.uk/news/article-2727090.
[2] 'They do Red Nose Day and send it to Africa but what about

1

Such stories are widespread in the media, playing to our prejudices and fomenting anger in our increasingly divided and secular society. In the past there was a widely accepted, if morally dubious, distinction between the deserving and the undeserving poor. This was clearly judgemental and often harsh in practice but at least it saw the need to offer support to those who had fallen on hard times through what was perceived to be no fault of their own. Today, it seems, even that distinction has been swept away. The jobless are simply idle; those who claim benefits are just scroungers. These are easy labels with which to classify and condemn whole sections of society but they do not tell the whole story nor do they address the hard questions as to how and why people become unemployed or homeless in the first place.

Partly in response to public outcry, politicians of all parties have wrestled for many years with the problem of how to deal with Britain's so-called under-class. They have tried introducing punitive measures such as building more prisons, issuing anti-social behaviour orders and making benefits harder to claim, none of which have had an impact on reducing crime. On the other hand, well-intentioned attempts to tackle the problems at source have also failed to produce the hoped-for results: those who have been in care, for instance, are still disproportionately highly represented in the statistics for unemployment, homelessness and criminality despite the extension of the state's responsibility from the age of 16 to 21.[3] Even the ambitious Troubled Families Programme, which specifically targeted 120,000 families across England with multiple problems, including

our country?'. Mother who rakes in £20k in handouts criticises system for refusing benefits to her Polish boyfriend': www. dailymail.co.uk/femail/article-3099563.

[3] www.prisonreformtrust.org.uk/ProjectsResearch/CareReview.

crime, anti-social behaviour, truancy, unemployment, mental health problems and domestic abuse, missed its key objectives. Despite costing £448 million and providing key workers to mentor such families regularly, the analysis of the first phase of the programme, which ran from 2012 to 2015, found that it had achieved 'no significant or systemic impact on outcomes related to employment, job seeking, school attendance, or anti-social behaviour'.[4]

If nothing works, then what are we to do? We can't ignore the problem and hope that it will just go away because, even if we ignore the moral imperative to act, at the most basic and selfish level the problem is one that affects us all socially and financially. There is, however, a different way. For 30 years one charity has consistently demonstrated that it is possible to change lives for the better profoundly and permanently. Year on year throughout those three decades Caring For Life has achieved at least 90% success rates in preventing a return to offending or homelessness; at the time of writing, of the 120 people currently being cared for in the community, not a single one has become homeless.[5] This is an astonishing record by any standard. The official statistics for England and Wales issued by the Department of Justice in 2015, for example, reveal that since 2004 prov-

---

[4] *Final Synthesis Report, National Evaluation of the first Troubled Families Programme 2012–2015*, published by the Department for Communities and Local Government on 17 Oct 2016, p. 69: www.gov.uk/government/publications/national-evaluation-of-the-first-troubled-families-programme. Nevertheless, the second phase, with a budget of £920 million and targeting an additional 400,000 families, went ahead in 2015 and will run until 2020: http://researchbriefings.parliament.uk/ResearchBriefing/Summary/CBP-7585.

[5] Of the 120 currently cared for (May 2017), 19 have offending records and two have reoffended: all figures supplied by Caring For Life.

en reoffending rates (which do not cover all reoffending) have remained between 25% and 27% and that within a year of being released from custody between 44.1% and 48.6% of adults have been convicted of further offences.[6] Homelessness statistics are more difficult to obtain as the government only releases official figures for statutory homelessness, a definition based on those who are accepted by their local authority as being owed the full rehousing duties, therefore the figures do not include anyone whose claims are rejected or who has not approached their local authority. Even so, the data suggests rising numbers of rough sleepers and, in London alone, a seven-fold increase between 2009/10 and 2014/15 in those becoming homeless at the end of a short term tenancy.[7] Against this background, Caring For Life's achievement shines all the more powerfully because the charity is often only brought in as a last resort when other agencies have failed to secure safe long-term housing for those who have been, or are at risk of being, evicted.

How and why does Caring For Life succeed so spectacularly where so many others have failed? There are two reasons, both simple in themselves but, at the same time, radically different from the mainstream approach. The first is that, as its name suggests, the charity offers care for life, not just for the three months to two years which is generally

[6] Proven reoffending is defined as an offence leading to a court conviction, caution, reprimand or warning which has been committed within a year of being released from custody, receiving a non-custodial conviction at court or receiving a reprimand or warning: www.gov.uk/government/statistics/proven-reoffending-statistics-july-2014-to-june-2015.

[7] www.publications.parliament.uk/pa/cm201617/cmselect/cmcomloc/40/4005.htm; see also www.londonspovertyprofile.org.uk/indicators/topics/homelessness/?gclid=COmzupiO4NMCF-cO37Qodfd0O8g.

the cut-off point for government funding. Agencies and charities which rely on such funding have to turn their clients' lives around within that brief window of opportunity or lose this source of income. Inevitably, therefore, it is the most damaged and vulnerable people, those whose needs cannot be addressed easily and quickly, who end up being passed from one agency to another. They are a liability since their problems are so deep-seated that simply providing them with accommodation and short-term support is not enough to break a cycle of behaviour which may have evolved and taken hold over many years. Other social care agencies understand this but they cannot continue to provide what is required once their own available funding ends. That is why so many of them refer their most needy clients to Caring For Life.

When someone is referred to Caring For Life, however, they become part of a family whose commitment to their needs is life-long. It can take years – sometimes many years – of patient encouragement and support to break down the mistrust and hostility of those who have been failed time and again by those who were supposed to care for them. While Caring For Life's objective is to enable them to live independent lives safely in their own homes and, where possible, to move into employment, there will always be those who cannot do so. Some will only need short periods of intensive help to enable them to stand on their own feet and give them the confidence to move forward, knowing that, at any time, they can come back again if the need or desire arises. Some will always be dependent on the regular home visits and support that Caring For Life's staff and volunteers offer year in and year out. Some who will never be able to live independently can find a home – a true home – for as long as they need or want it in one of Caring For

Life's two supported homes for eight ladies and eight gentlemen. Whatever the level of need and whenever it arises, Caring For Life will be there. It is no coincidence that when the outreach team working in the community was looking for a name it was the very people who have benefited from its care who christened it the 'Being There' team. Many of their stories are told in this book.

Even more important than the promise of life-long care, however, is the second reason for Caring For Life's success: an absolute and unswerving commitment to the Christian principles upon which it was founded. Jesus Christ embraced society's untouchables and offered unconditional love to its outcasts – the poor, the homeless, the sick in mind and body – and, in so doing, he transformed their lives. This is the example that Caring For Life aspires to follow, reaching out particularly to the homeless and vulnerable, treating them with the dignity and respect which is due to those who have been created in God's own image and fostering in them a sense of self-worth upon which to build a new life and identity. These objectives are summed up in Caring For Life's motto, 'Sharing the Love of Jesus', which underpins everything it does. Though the charity cares for people of all faiths and none, every member of staff and volunteer is personally pledged to fulfil the commandment that Jesus himself gave to those who follow him: 'Love one another. As I have loved you, so you must love one another. By this everyone will know that you are my disciples, if you love one another'.[8]

For this reason Caring For Life gives far more than most other services can provide. Ensuring physical safety and well-being is just a first step, not an end in itself. Addressing mental health problems, which range from depression and

---

[8] John 13.34–35: New International Version.

agoraphobia to complex psychological issues, often caused by physical, mental and sexual abuse from childhood, is more difficult but it is key to changing lives. Sometimes it is as simple as befriending those who lead chaotic lives, ensuring that they attend their doctor's appointments, understand and remember to order their medication and have someone who cares about them to whom they can talk in confidence. More often than not, however, it takes many years of building trust and demonstrating by personal example the truth of the apostle Paul's description of the nature of Christian love: 'Love is patient, love is kind. It does not envy, it does not boast, it is not proud. It does not dishonour others, it is not self-seeking, it is not easily angered, it keeps no record of wrongs. Love does not delight in evil but rejoices with the truth. It always protects, always trusts, always hopes, always perseveres'.[9]

It is not always easy to offer such unconditional love to anyone, let alone to people who have never experienced anything but rejection and abuse and are therefore hurting, angry, even overtly hostile. Crag House Farm, the home of Caring For Life, plays a fundamental supportive role in helping to achieve this by providing opportunities to change lives. It is an extraordinary place where even the most casual visitor cannot fail to sense the profound peace and spirituality which permeates what might otherwise appear to be just another working farm. Yet it is here that some of the most damaged and anti-social people are to be found, either engaged in one of the many daytime therapeutic projects, which range from looking after the farm animals to lessons in literacy and numeracy, confiding their troubles in the quiet of the sensory gardens, or simply enjoying a meal, company and laughter in the centre. The farm is a

---

[9] 1 Corinthians 13.4–7: New International Version.

vibrant community and, by its very existence, draws in and embraces those who have spent their lives being excluded. For many of them this will be their first experience of genuine friendship – and what is perhaps most moving of all is the fact that this Christian fellowship is also offered by those who are being cared for themselves. They have learned by example. As one of them, who, over a number of years, had been among the most disruptive and difficult to help, said, when explaining his own act of unsolicited kindness to a homeless man he met on the streets, 'I have learnt from the best'.

The stories of some of these people and the transformative experience they have undergone form the subject of this book. All their names have been changed to protect the identity of vulnerable individuals and families, some of whom have been with Caring For Life since its inception in 1987. I regret that this means I have not been able to give the true names of some of the charity's beneficiaries who would have been proud to be included in these pages and have frequently asked me if their stories will appear here. It is also a matter of personal regret that limitations of space have prevented me from being able to name, or even include, so many long-serving members of staff and volunteers who have 'worked tirelessly and loved relentlessly' over the last 30 years. Without them the charity could not have survived, let alone reached out to so many vulnerable, hurting people and changed so many lives. Lack of space has also obliged me to omit mention of many of those charitable individuals, organisations and grant-making trusts whose generosity has underpinned the work of Caring For Life and enabled it to continue and grow. My sins of omission, however, do not reflect the incalculable debt of gratitude owed by the charity, and those it cares for, to each and every one of its supporters, no matter how great or small the contribution they have made.

For the full story of how the charity began and evolved over the first 20 years of its existence readers are referred to my previous book *The Deafening Sound of Silent Tears* (Canterbury Press, 2007). This new work, *Drops into an Ocean*, is published to celebrate the thirtieth anniversary of the foundation of Caring For Life and all profits from its sale will again be given to the charity. It might seem surprising that another decade justifies a whole new book but there have been dramatic developments over the last ten years which have both challenged and changed the way Caring For Life operates. Visitors to Crag House Farm in 2007 would hardly recognise the place as it is today. The buildings may be different but what remains unchanged is Caring For Life's unwavering commitment to 'Sharing the love of Jesus' with all those people it encounters on a daily basis. It is a commitment which, as we shall see, has come at considerable cost, both personal and financial, but it is also the reason that Caring For Life has survived through difficult times and seen its work blessed above and beyond all human expectations. In the wonderful words of the psalmist, which are now engraved on the entrance to the Granary restaurant and farm shop, 'Not to us, Lord, not to us but to your name be the glory.'[10]

---

[10] Psalm 115.1: New International Version

2
Forward in Faith

'Let me share with you some of the things that I hope we will be able to accomplish during 2007', Peter Parkinson, the co-founder of Caring For Life, announced on the twentieth anniversary of the charity's foundation. 'We want to begin and complete our new Adult Learning Centre, which is this year's priority building project, but we would also love to commence the restoration of our 17th century barn ... [and] we must complete the refurbishment of our kitchen for the Catering Academy.' That was not all, however. A new and better meat preparation room was a necessity because the existing one would be lost when building work began on the Adult Learning Centre. To complete the list, an all-weather facility for the Equestrian Project would be 'enormously helpful'. It might take five or even ten years to accomplish all these projects, Peter said, but most of them needed to begin immediately and to be completed before the summer of 2008.

This was an extraordinarily ambitious agenda, as Peter himself was the first to admit. It was also one which just 20 years earlier he would have found impossible even to imagine, let alone put into effect. Caring For Life had started out as an impromptu response to the needs of a group of troubled local teenagers. As the pastor of Leeds Reformed Baptist Church and official visitor to Foxcroft, a local authority children's home, Peter had witnessed at first hand the growing problem facing young people who, at that time, generally had to leave the care system at the age of just 16. Lacking the life skills necessary for independent living, and often still suffering from the mental health problems caused by childhood abuse or neglect which had necessitated their being taken into care in the first place, increasing numbers of them were unable to find or keep employment, were rapidly becoming homeless and even drifting into criminality. Some of these young men were well-known to both Peter and members of his congregation, particularly Esther Smith, who had been housemother at Foxcroft, and Wendy Pollard, her principal assistant. Having loved 'her boys' throughout their years of care, Esther could not bear to see them abandoned now simply because they were considered old enough to look after themselves. 'Somebody ought to do something about this!' she insisted to Peter during one of many heated discussions on the subject. 'What can *I* do?' was his natural response. To which Esther replied (jabbing her finger in his chest as Peter remembers it, though Esther denies it) 'Everyone says that! But we can do *something*, no matter how small. If all of us do *something*, then it *will* make a difference, no matter how small.'

And so Caring For Life was born out of a desire to make a difference. It was a measure of how small that difference was expected to be that its first home was loaned by a member of the congregation; volunteers from the church helped to provide the furniture and furnishings and also acted as unpaid residential staff each night. Carey House opened its doors on 28th February 1987 to four deeply damaged young men, some of whom are still supported, to varying degrees, by Caring For Life 30 years later. Carey House provided the model for the charity's provision of future accommodation in that it was emphatically a home, not a hostel. The privacy of its residents was to be respected at all times:

visitors had to be invited in as guests not just into the bed-rooms but into the home itself – a principle some of the young men struggled with at first, most of them having always lived in institutional care and been accustomed to having nowhere that belonged to them alone.

What Peter, Esther and their small group of Christians had not fully anticipated when they originally founded Caring For Life was the sheer scale of the problem they had tentatively set out to address. In the few short weeks before Carey House was ready to open they had received more than 80 applications for the four places available. In the face of such overwhelming need, there could only be one response: to move forward in faith. Five months later a second home, Tindall House, was opened in two adjoining properties loaned by Leeds City Council because they were scheduled for demolition in three years' time. Even this new provision could not begin to match the need, however, so a different approach was also required. Esther became an intermediary, contacting the city's Housing Department to help find local authority accommodation for those young people who needed it but were unable to navigate their way through the system to access it for themselves. Caring For Life's volunteers would then help to ensure that tenancies were maintained by visiting regularly to offer both friendship and practical support. This was the mustard seed from which would spring the mighty tree that is the Being There team today.

From the very beginning Caring For Life was never just about providing housing and Crag House Farm, on the outskirts of Leeds, was already an integral part of the charity's commitment to life long care. Originally just the home of Peter Parkinson and his family, it had been a much-loved playground for the Foxcroft children: now it would also provide a taste of the countryside and offer a safe haven for young adults who had never known anything other than the urban deprivation and tensions of inner-city life. Unless they were in paid employment or attending college, all those who lived in the homes were encouraged to come to the farm so that they could help to tend the vegetable plots and to look after the goats, chickens and horses. In doing so, they learned transferable skills which might lead to employment, including the ability to turn up on time each day and to take responsibility for the welfare of plants and animals which were dependent on them for survival. Perhaps more importantly, they also developed their capacity for social and emotional engagement with their mentors and with each other, working side-by-side in the calm surroundings of the farm projects and letting off steam by playing football together in the hours devoted to recreational activity. Inspired by the example of those who looked after them, some would begin to attend church and ultimately come to faith. 'I wasn't a Christian before I came to Caring For Life', Aaron testifies. 'I needed help. No one cared about me and I was homeless for a while ... I lived at Carey House and now I'm at Tindall House ... Having a family at Caring For Life and a safe home is great, but knowing Jesus is even better.'

There were many times over the first two decades when Caring For Life seems to have survived on the power of prayer alone. It was a hand-to-mouth existence, never knowing when – or if – money would be available to provide even the most basic needs. Yet the demand was importunate and growing. Loaned properties had to be returned and were eventually replaced with permanent homes owned and run by the charity: the new Tindall House for eight gentlemen opened in December 1990 and Wendy Margaret Home for eight ladies in March 2001, both purchases made possible only with the aid of charitable trusts and gifts from generous individual Christian supporters and churches. To provide continuity of care, as well as to improve and expand in the face of an ever-increasing work load, it became necessary to employ paid staff, rather than rely solely on volunteers. Funding salaries became (and remains) a major financial pressure, not least because most grant-makers prefer to fund projects rather than on-going costs. There have been occasions when staff had to be made redundant; at other times they have been asked to take a temporary reduction in their wages to enable their work to continue. Such sacrifices would be unacceptable in any other workplace, but Caring For Life is no ordinary organisation and its staff are not just employees, but Christians committed to a life-changing mission. Without them, and the equally sacrificial giving of time and money by volunteers and supporters over the years, it is hard to see how the charity could have survived, let alone grown. As Peter said in 2007, when looking back over the previous 20 years, 'It seems miraculous to me that we are still here! But through many trials, many dangers, in spite of numerous mistakes on our part, by the grace of God we are still here and still sharing the love of Jesus with anyone who comes within the parameters of our care or who comes, for whatever reason, to visit us here at Crag House Farm.'

It was an achievement in itself simply to have kept going for so long in the face of so many difficulties but standing still was not an option. More people than ever before were now being referred to Caring For Life and though the daily projects at the farm had expanded to cater for them, this placed new pressures on the charity's resources. The ancient barn where the Longhorn cattle were over-wintered was becoming unfit for purpose and no longer a safe place for vulnerable people to be in close contact with such large animals, despite the important pastoral benefits of them being able to do so. Most of the therapeutic activities, including the very popular Music and Drama Projects, as well as the Catering Academy, had to compete for time and space in the same building, a converted scout hut, which also housed the charity's kitchen. As this was where everyone gathered for meals and tea breaks, all activities had to stop and everything cleared away several times a day to allow the tables and chairs to be set out and food served. This raised health and safety issues but also placed frustrating limits on what could be done in the time available for the projects and the number of people who could be included.

Inspired by the words of William Carey, 'expect great things from God; attempt great things for God', the executive team decided that radical solutions were needed. It was time to move forward in faith once again and the twentieth anniversary of the charity's foundation was the appropriate moment to launch plans for the most ambitious building projects Caring For Life had ever undertaken. It fell to Peter, as chief executive, to explain why they were necessary. 'Because as Christians we want to provide the best we are able for those in our care; we want to provide facilities to enable the many therapeutic activities, which have achieved such remarkable success, to develop and grow in the safest environment ... We want people to look at Caring For Life and recognise that God will honour those who honour him ... We want people to come to this place and whisper, "Surely God is here!"'.

The new Adult Learning Centre was to be built within a former fold yard, creating dedicated rooms for the Literacy and Numeracy, Music, Drama and Arts and Crafts

Projects. An existing stone barn would be adapted to extend the space for the Computer and Media Project but also to accommodate Caring For Life's first commercial enterprise on the farm premises which would be open to the public. The Granary café would serve breakfasts and lunches to showcase the quality of Caring For Life's produce – the home-grown meat, eggs and salads, together with a new range of chutneys, herb jellies, jams and fruit vinegars made on the farm mainly from the Conservation Project harvest and all be available for sale in the café's small farm shop. It was hoped that the café would provide a new and regular stream of income, not just from the sale of food and drink, but also by publicising the charity's work and therefore attracting donations and increasing its supporter base. Grouped around a small, sunny courtyard, the new range of buildings would provide a private, safe and quiet space for all those visiting the farm to enjoy, whether as beneficiaries taking part in the therapeutic activities, or customers dining in what was swiftly nicknamed 'the glass box'.

Many charitable trusts were keen to support this type of social enterprise with its proven record of success and at least two substantial donations towards the cost were also made by generous individuals. By June 2007 it was possible to begin preliminary work on replacing the barn's corrugated metal roof with traditional stone tiles (an unwanted extra expense but a condition of the planning permission because it is a listed building) and on 21st June, the charity's much-loved patron, HRH The Countess of Wessex, laid the foundation stone of the new Adult Learning Centre. Another giant step forward in faith had been taken.

By the summer of 2007 it seemed as if the whole of Crag House Farm was a building site. In addition to all the work on the Adult Learning Centre and Granary café, the kitchens in the centre had been completely refurbished and a new food storage facility added; a huge new agricultural barn, dubbed the PAM (People and Animals Meeting) building, was being constructed to improve the housing and handling of sheep and cattle but also to provide a safe environment for those working alongside them; the workshops were being extended to house the new tack room and lockers for the Equestrian Project as well as a much-needed laundry; and the Woodwork Project, helped by volunteers, had built a new potting shed to provide shelter and storage for those working on the Horticultural Project.

In the midst of all this activity, the reason why it was all so necessary was powerfully brought home by the desperate plight of some of those in the charity's care. Alison was in her mid-thirties when she decided to end her life. She had a long history of mental health problems, including self-harming, and struggled to cope with the additional burdens of epilepsy, alcoholism and a violent partner. Her children had been removed from her and she was not allowed to look after them. With nothing left to live for, and overwhelmed by the pain of her existence, she had again tried to kill herself, this time by pouring petrol over her head and setting herself on fire. Tragically, though her life was saved, her failed attempt left her even worse off than before: her thumbs and fingers on both hands were completely destroyed and she was so badly scarred that she lost much of her facial mobility and was unable to walk properly. Her mental scars went even deeper. Her Caring For Life supporter continued to visit her regularly, helped her move into a new flat and, 18 months after that terrible day, brought her back to the farm so that, at Alison's own request, she could see the horses. She was encouraged to attend the Equestrian Project and to some extent managed to rebuild her life. Five years after her suicide attempt, however, she unexpectedly collapsed and died of natural causes. Her tragedy was a reminder to everyone at Caring For Life of how little could be done to help someone so deeply damaged, but that that little was better than nothing. At her funeral there was also an opportunity to reach out to her family, particularly her little boy who had been traumatised by witnessing his mother's sufferings and terrible scarring. He had written her a private letter, telling her how much he loved her, and became increasingly upset that he was unable to give it to her. Peter promised to deliver it and, with the aid of the crematorium staff, was able to place it in her coffin and so comfort the poor boy with the knowledge that his mother had, indeed, received his letter.

Alison's story was particularly shocking but her situation was by no means unusual. Another lady in her late thirties, who, from the age of three, had been subjected to terrible physical and sexual abuse at the hands of various members of her family, including her father and mother, and others, eventually found sanctuary in Wendy Margaret Home. She quickly responded to the kindness and care shown her by becoming visibly happier and healthier, but it took her a year and a half for her to acquire the confidence to tell Esther that her abuse still continued every time she visited her family home. She had not dared to cut herself off from her abusers completely because they had threatened that her own child would suffer in her place if she refused to comply or if she disclosed what was happening.

Given that so many abusive situations of this kind are hidden from public view within the sufferers' own homes and families, it is not surprising that many of those whom Caring For Life looks after struggle with the concept that anyone should care about them at all. When Peter asked a group of young people who had gathered for a Bible study session what they understood by the word 'Father' he was met with looks of incomprehension: the concept of a loving father was completely outside their experience. And when one, who had come from a happy Christian home, suggested that a father was someone who 'looks after and cares for you', he received the swift and bitter response from Adam, 'Not always.'

This same young man had suffered such violence and abuse at the hands of his father that he had arrived at Caring For Life unable to speak or make eye contact with anyone. Until he became a Christian, he said, the happiest day of his life had been when he heard that his father was dead. Gradually, however, his life was transformed by Caring For Life and, through grace and the example of those who cared for him, he had come to faith.[11] Just how far he had changed was demonstrated at his sister's funeral. She, too, had been a victim of their father's vicious cruelty and, although she had also become a Christian, gained many friends and held a responsible job, she had struggled to cope with the legacy of depression that haunted her. A failed relationship triggered two suicide attempts and, two months later, while on the waiting list for psychotherapy, she succeeded in killing herself, at the age of 37, by jumping from the roof of a multi-storey carpark. The circumstances of her death were devastating for all who had known her but Caring For Life sought to support her remaining family. One of Adam's other sisters had been determined to give her own little eulogy at the funeral. When she stood up to do so, however, she was completely overcome with grief and unable to proceed. It was Adam himself who took the eulogy from

---

[11] Adam's poignant story can be found in *The Deafening Sound of Silent Tears*, pp.19–21, 27.

her, read it out, then gently escorted her back to her seat and sat with her for the rest of the service. Sensitive, loving, supportive behaviour, the absolute antithesis of the way he had been brought up, but of the kind that can blossom in even the most damaged people when the love of Jesus is shared with them.

Broken lives are never mended easily or quickly yet the window of opportunity to help is often frustratingly small. Dinah, a Wendy Margaret Home resident who had been abused from early childhood, was at considerable risk of self-harm and, in her darker moments, would claim that she had taken a massive overdose. Each claim had to be taken seriously, necessitating urgent trips to hospital. After several incidents of this kind, the hospital referred her to a specialist psychiatric unit where her medication was changed and she was told she would have to become an in-patient for a while. It was heart-breaking for the staff at Caring For Life to see the effect this had on a woman who had become so actively involved in Music, Equestrian and Horticultural Projects, was learning new skills in the Catering Academy and, for the first time, was beginning to look forward to the future with excitement at the prospect of a projected trip to America. Within 48 hours of hospitalisation and with nothing to do except sit in her ward, smoking and watching television, Dinah once again became withdrawn and deeply depressed. When she eventually decided not to return to Wendy Margaret Home, the only comfort for those who had cared for her was that she was not reverting completely to her former life: however briefly, she had experienced unconditional love and she knew that Caring For Life would always be there for her if ever she wanted to come back home again.

While always hoping for miracles, Caring For Life has

inevitably had to accept that some deeply damaged and vulnerable people will never break the chains that bind them to their abusive pasts. Each and every failure is hugely painful and some staff and volunteers can feel overwhelmed by the scale of the problems facing the individuals in their care. Most find the strength and faith to persevere, rewarded by the knowledge that their ministry is so desperately needed. As Peter himself put it, 'There are few things more fulfilling than knowing that you are genuinely, really and desperately needed. The things we are doing are what the God of all the earth has called and commissioned us to do.'

Sometimes, however, the faith of even the most committed supporter of Caring For Life can be tested to its limits. In the midst of the biggest building programme in the charity's existence, some of its most important sources of large-scale finance were being closed off, in some cases because of its Christian ethos. After long and very difficult negotiations, Leeds City Council eventually agreed to extend its Supporting People funding for three years but no further, raising the prospect that both the homes and the outreach work in the community would soon lose a sizeable tranche of their income. Grant-making trusts were under increasing social and political pressure to end what was believed to be the discriminatory practice of supporting purely Christian charities. Even if an application for a donation 'ticked all the boxes' in terms of a trust's objectives, and would make an immense difference in enabling Caring For Life to support more people, the words 'sharing the love of Jesus' in the charity's mission statement were now deemed unacceptable by some trusts who refused to make a grant unless they were removed. Since this was equally unacceptable to Caring For Life, the charity could no longer hope to obtain future grants from such grant-makers. A trustee of another charity, which did in fact contribute a grant towards the Adult Learning Centre, later visited the farm and complained that 'It is obvious that your Christian faith pervades everything you do, and if we had known you were Christians we would never have supported you, nor would we support Jews or Muslims.'[12] Caring For Life's already heavy reliance on its Christian support base – individuals and churches as well as charities – would have to become even greater.

It therefore seemed particularly bad timing that an un-expected opportunity now arose to purchase an additional 40 acres of land adjoining Crag House Farm. A neighbour-ing farmer offered the charity first option to buy her fields which lay between the farm and Otley Old Road. This was providential because it had been a condition of the planning consent for the Adult Learning Centre that every means possible should be explored to replace the old dirt track which linked the farm to the nearest main road, a route that also passed through a housing estate. Here, was the obvious answer. Buying the land offered a unique opportunity to create a new access road and also to expand the Agricultur-al Project by increasing the amount of lamb and beef pro-duced, thereby helping Caring For Life to become more financially self-reliant and reducing its dependence on gov-ernment funding. But the cost was huge: £410,000 for the land alone and an additional £40,000 to create the road.

In the midst of seeking to fund so many other building commitments, it seemed impossible that the money could be found. Jonathan Parkinson, Peter's son, who was accom-panying some of the charity's beneficiaries on holiday in America at the time, was therefore astonished when he was woken by a telephone call from his father in the middle of

[12] That Caring For Life is a Christian ministry is always explicit-ly set out in all its literature, including grant applications and annual reports.

the night to tell him that a supporter had just offered to give Caring For Life the entire sum required to purchase the land. So incredible did this seem that, next morning, he told Peter about his wonderful dream, only to be informed that it was in fact completely true. The donation was in response to an appeal in the monthly bulletin which also produced a flood of other generous offers so that, by the end of its twentieth anniversary year, Caring For Life was able to agree to buy the land outright and plan the new access road. Peter's grateful acknowledgement of this often deeply sacrificial giving also contained a humble admission. 'I do believe that the Lord can do all things, I do believe that he hears and answers prayers, but I never expect miracles such as the response of so many of you at this time. I need your and the Lord's forgiveness for my lack of faith.'

To crown a year of extraordinary challenges matched by equal blessings, Caring For Life learned just before Christmas that Dunbia Meats, a supplier of high quality beef and lamb products based in Northern Ireland, had offered not only to build a new meat preparation and processing room but also to provide ongoing expert advice and support in every aspect of the project, including quality control, production and marketing. It was yet another opportunity to transform the charity's facilities, involving more vulnerable people in its activities and contributing towards earning the income to sustain its mission. There was a palpable sense of anticipation and change in the air, neatly encapsulated by one of the trustees, Neil Deacon: 'I genuinely believe that 20 years from now we will look back and say, "That year, 2007, was a turning point." And I think that is the most exciting thing I have felt for quite some time about Caring For Life.'

3

Building for the Future

Despite all the disruption and distraction caused by the building work the needs of the damaged and vulnerable people looked after by Caring For Life remained its priority. Many months of planning and saving by all those involved culminated in a very special holiday for 16 of them. Accompanied by nine staff and volunteers, they spent two and a half weeks touring California in five enormous camper vans, visiting some of the natural wonders of the world from Death Valley to the Grand Canyon (described as 'a hole in the ground' by one of them) but also taking in Disneyland and Universal Studios. It was a huge undertaking in terms of preparing and packing all the medication needed for the 24 hour journey, calming those with learning difficulties who were anxious or volatile and shepherding them all safely round the sites but, with the aid of their supporters and hosts at Grace Providence Church in Cerritos, fantastic memories were created for people whose lives had hitherto been bereft of anything they wanted to remember. And there were moving moments of prayer, shared with their American friends, which demonstrated that even those who did not attend church had felt the power of God's love in the wonders of His creation. Esther noted that it was those who had been longest with Caring For Life who were the most observant and appreciative of all the natural beauties they had seen: the delightful Californian bluebirds, the starry skies over Death Valley, the dolphins playing in the surf on Huntingdon Beach.

Caring For Life's outreach team had been busy supporting 138 people to live out in the community. Despite 2007 being just a typical year, it was a graphic illustration of the level of need that among that group alone there had been 127 'dire crises' over the year, including sleeping rough, bereavement, violence from a partner, severe self-harm, unlawful eviction, relationship breakdown and addiction. 64 individuals were helped to find emergency accommodation and for one 80 year-old gentleman struggling to live on his own there was a wonderful surprise when, having been whisked away to enjoy a day out, he returned to find that all the jobs he had been worrying about but unable to do himself had been done for him. His kitchen, bathroom and lounge had been repainted, a new carpet laid and a newly acquired suite installed. It was an experience he would never forget, not just because his life had been made more comfortable, but because it showed how deeply others cared about him. At Christmas, which is often a particularly difficult period for isolated, impoverished and vulnerable people, the team delivered more than 120 presents to individuals and families, many of whom would receive nothing else, and, despite the fact that the farm was still a building site, 46 of them came there to enjoy the usual Christmas parties and festivities. Again, this was an opportunity to build happy memories for those who had so few to recall, but also to introduce them to the real meaning of Christmas by sharing the love of Jesus with them at this precious time.

As always seems to be the case with building work, there were delays and, more seriously, costs began to escalate and problems multiply. The existing utility services proved to be inadequate for the additional needs of the new buildings, requiring an improved electricity supply and a new water pipe from the main road which, fortunately, was less difficult than it might have been, thanks to the recent acquisition of the new fields. The budgeted cost of the new road across the same land, however, had increased substantially due to planning regulations.

Throughout the spring and summer of 2008, Caring For Life demonstrated once again the truth of St Francis's exhortation, 'Begin by doing what is necessary, then do what is possible, and pretty soon you are doing the impossible!' It was through grace alone that the impossible was achieved when the farm held its annual Open Day on 21st June 2008 and supporters were able to see for themselves the transformation that had been achieved. The new PAM building had been ready in time to bring in the sheep for lambing, its all-important safe-handling facilities enabling those on the Agricultural Project to become intimately involved in the daily care of, and responsibility for, animals which are dependent on them. It is always a joy to see someone who has always felt useless and ignored respond with pride and pleasure when an animal chooses to come to them, even if it is only in the hope of food. It is also deeply moving to see people who have never received any affection themselves hugging a lamb, helping a new-born calf or simply giving a comforting head-rub to one of the intimidatingly large Longhorn cattle. Touring the new facility on Open Day under their expert and often voluble guidance it was obvious how great a contribution it was going to make to the farm and also, more importantly, to those taking part in the Agricultural Project. (Though one supporter did rather regret trying to draw out a hitherto quiet young man by asking him about the bull and receiving a rather too graphic account of its purpose and activities!)

On Open Day supporters were also able to visit the new

Adult Learning Centre for the first time and admire the purpose-built rooms and their high quality fittings which were such a contrast to the former cramped and comparatively shabby quarters of the various activities. The adult Literacy and Numeracy Project, where lives would be transformed simply by being taught to read and write; the Computer and Media Project, where modern technology skills would be taught and put to immediate practical use in producing a website and the monthly bulletins, films and DVDs for supporters; the Music and Drama Project, where withdrawn, unhappy people with learning difficulties or speech impediments would find a means to express themselves and experience the delight of entertaining others; the Art and Craft Project, which had been unable to operate for two years due to lack of space and would now buzz with purposeful creative activity in its own large and light-filled room.

Those who had had the vision and courage to take such an enormous step – or rather leap – forward in faith to bring all these new projects to fruition had never looked for more than the reward of knowing that they were walking in the Master's footsteps but it was also a great encouragement to have the universal approbation of the supporters who had gathered there that day. Around a thousand of them had travelled from every corner of the UK and more than a hundred churches were represented at the opening service. A day of great blessing was marred only by pouring rain. For an autistic resident of Tindall House, who had always successfully prayed for good weather each Open Day, this was both bewildering and upsetting. Why had God failed to deliver? One of his fellow residents, who had only recently come to faith himself, had the answer: 'God must have had a reason! It didn't stop any of our supporters coming, did it? But it did stop the public, those people who aren't our supporters, didn't it? It was just the Caring For Life family who came, wasn't it? That's great, isn't it!'

Open Day also saw a highly successful launch of the Granary café and farm shop: there were long queues for the 20 places available, the staff and volunteers were run off their feet and the shelves of the shop were rapidly emptied of all their home-produced stock. The café would soon build up a regular clientele and, in doing so, opened up a new and unexpected area of ministry. Visitors found that they enjoyed the simple but superb quality of the fresh food and they were made to feel genuinely welcome. Serving staff and volunteers would always make time for a friendly chat but would also go that extra step further in offering a sympathetic ear to those who wished to share their troubles. Many of the customers were elderly and lonely; some were recently bereaved or suffering from life-threatening illnesses themselves; others were worn down by the daily burden of caring for beloved relatives with physical or mental disabilities. The Granary café was, and is, a place where all are made to feel welcome, accepted and comfortable, from nursing mothers to those with mobility problems or multiple and complex needs. Knowing that you can spend a quiet hour or two away from the pressures of daily life can be deeply restorative. It can also be a joy to feel able to include loved ones in a family celebration, even if they have dementia or other challenging behaviour which might be frowned upon in a more 'normal' café. Whether visitors understand it or not – and many do – this is a practical way of sharing the love of Jesus with them. Even those who come just to enjoy a good meal in the company of friends can take satisfaction from the fact that every penny of profit from their patronage is helping to support the vital work of Caring For Life among those less fortunate than themselves.

The fact that the little café and shop were so successful was to become increasingly important because by the late summer of 2008 the whole country, and indeed most of the world, was in the grip of a financial crisis of terrifying proportions. As international banks failed or were bailed out by governments and their tax-payers, stock markets plunged in value, the housing market collapsed and credit became extremely hard to get. For Caring For Life, in the midst of the biggest expansion in its history, the consequences were potentially disastrous. Loans for the PAM building and completion of the Adult Learning Centre had to be serviced or repaid. Grants from charitable trusts and foundations provided up to 15% of its annual income but their ability to make future grants would be severely limited by their own falling investment income. Most crucially of all, many of those Christian individuals whose long and faithful support had always been the charity's most important source of income, were forced by their own financial difficulties to reduce or even end their giving.

Yet the desperate need among the poor and vulnerable remained and increased as the global financial crisis deepened. Every day new people were being referred to Caring For Life. One homeless lady was frail and elderly. Devoted to her two sons, she would not hear a word against them, even though it was their violent behaviour that had led to their being evicted so many times that most housing agencies were now unwilling to accept her and, as a result, she had been living in a hostel for over a year. Even there her two sons continued to abuse her, threatening and beating her until, yet again, she gave them all her money. It was not until she finally admitted that it was one of her sons who was responsible for her latest extensive bruising and asked

Caring For Life to protect her that it was possible to apply for an urgent court injunction that, by keeping her sons away from her, would make it easier to help her find accommodation.

Another elderly lady with many problems of her own was also the sole carer for her son who was highly gifted but struggled with the ordinary tasks of everyday life such as going on a bus or to the shops. Caring For Life had supported them for some time, offering practical help such as refitting their dilapidated kitchen, sorting out the overgrown garden and installing a new secure front door, but what really made the difference in both their lives was when Barnabus started to attend the Art and Craft Project. From being totally isolated and withdrawn he now found friendship and encouragement but also rediscovered his enthusiasm for drawing which gave him a new interest in life and transformed his sense of self-worth. Barnabus was just one of many new people now able to take part in the Art and Craft, Music and Drama Projects on a weekly basis as a result of the enhanced facilities offered by the new Adult Learning Centre.

This was a cause for much thanksgiving and was duly celebrated in style in September 2008 when HRH The Countess of Wessex paid another visit to the farm for the formal opening of the Adult Learning Centre and the PAM building, making her entrance along the new access road which had been completed just in time for her arrival. The countess's visits to the farm are always a great encouragement to staff and supporters and create much anticipation and excitement among those they look after. Everyone wants to dress up for the occasion and hopes to get a chance to speak to her because she makes a point of engaging with as many of them as she can and does so with great empathy and understanding. To calm nerves and avoid any disasters on the day, there are usually practices for those who will be introduced. On one occasion, the volunteer playing the role of the countess, who knew them all well, made the mistake of calling Andrew 'Adam'. Andrew was suitably indignant so, in a misguided attempt to soothe his ruffled pride by turning the tables, she asked him what he would call her and was mortified when he promptly replied 'Leech!' Only later did she discover that this not a particularly barbed insult but actually a compliment, since that was the surname of the foster-mother to whom he had been closest. Fortunately the countess was spared this misunderstanding and all went well on the day.

During her visit the previous summer she had been highly entertained by a sample of one of Caring For Life's revues, which showcase the many extraordinary talents of those who are cared for, and asked them to repeat it at a fund-raising dinner that evening. So potential donors to the building programme were treated to everything from Aaron's beautiful singing of 'I'll fly away' to an excerpt from *A Midsummer Night's Dream* by the Drama Project, not to mention the hilarious morris-dancing sketch which had once prompted a bewildered observer to ask 'Which one is the autistic one?'. As the countess had clearly recognised, there could not have been a more powerful example of the way that Caring For Life so successfully reaches out and transforms broken lives and this impromptu Royal Command performance undoubtedly contributed to the success of the appeal for funds. A year later, many of those who had contributed so generously to the appeal were presented to the countess and personally thanked for their contribution. Among them were representatives of the 66 trusts (out of the 523 to whom applications were made) who, between them, had donated an amazing £556,884 towards the capital costs of the Adult Learning Centre. A wonderful day was marred only by the fact that one of the key figures was missing from the celebrations. Esther Smith was seriously ill in hospital with a viral infection. It was typical of the countess's deep personal involvement in all the people at Caring For Life that, much to the consternation of her security team, she insisted on paying Esther an unscheduled visit and spent 30 minutes at her bedside.

Esther's illness was undoubtedly caused in part by exhaustion and stress: she had borne the brunt of getting the Granary café and shop up and running to the extent that she was spending every hour available outside her usual heavy workload in making and preparing food. The appointment of a professional chef, Pete Washburn, would help to ease that burden but it would be several months before Esther was fit enough to return to work. There were other pressures too. Heavy snowfalls in the spring meant that, for the first time, the Granary began to lose money because customers did not want to venture out in the treacherous conditions. More seriously, some staff and beneficiaries were also unable to get to the farm, leaving the latter isolated and vulnerable without the stimulus of the daytime projects.

Perhaps as a result of the charity's raised public profile, these months also saw the farm repeatedly targeted by thieves and vandals. The gates on the new road were stolen and then the newly built dry-stone walls at the entrance were demolished and the stone placed across the drive to make it impassable. On one occasion barbed wire was strung across the road and on another someone actually dug a trench across the entrance and inserted a spiked steel plate to puncture tyres. Such incidents were extremely worrying both because of the potential danger to the drivers, motorcyclists and horses using the road and because they were clearly not just casual acts of thoughtless vandalism: they suggested a wilful determination to cause physical harm to people at the farm. The local police were extremely supportive, as always, offering help and advice on improving security and making regular visits which turned out to have an unexpected benefit. Many of those in Caring For Life's care have been petty criminals and some have convictions for more serious crimes. They have therefore always regarded the police with suspicion, if not active dislike. Now, however, they were forced to realise that these officers had become their protectors and were actively caring for them. It was a salutary lesson and a God-given opportunity to rethink attitudes and relationships.

As the global financial crisis deepened, Caring For Life was compelled to adapt to changing circumstances. Six members of staff were made redundant, a cause of great distress to everyone, including those attending the projects on which they had worked whom they had befriended and who were always nervous of change. All the remaining staff took a pay cut and many were reassigned to additional roles to share out the burden of the workload borne by those who had left. Staff were also personally challenged to raise £1000 each, leading to a whole raft of innovative fund-raising activities, including a highly successful exhibition and sale of work produced by supporters and some of those on the Art and Craft Project. For the latter, especially, it was very exciting to see that their artwork had merit and was valued by others; perhaps more importantly, they could feel that they were genuinely making their own contribution to help those who had helped them. A fund raising concert scheduled to take place outside in the courtyard in July was blessed in the most extraordinary way. The weather forecast predicted heavy rain and a call to the Met Office confirmed that it would be definitely be raining by 6pm. All the performers gathered that afternoon to pray that it would hold off until the concert had finished but by 6pm the storm clouds were gathering. The concert started: no rain. The interval overran by 20 minutes: still no rain. The concert ended at 9.30pm and its organiser Joanna then explained to the audience how their prayers had been answered. Just as the cheers rang out in response, the rain began to fall: ten minutes later it had become a downpour.

In the midst of all the financial difficulties there were many other answers to prayer. Unable to afford the hire of a marquee for the annual Open Day, the service for supporters was held instead in the PAM building which proved to be a much better venue as it was at the heart of the farm and its activities. The sheep and lambs waiting for the shearing demonstration made their presence felt with constant interruptions that caused much amusement. (The following year it was the turn of the Longhorn bull who let out an indignant – and perfectly timed – bellow when the Meat Project's beef burgers were mentioned.) The savings on the marquee hire, combined with record sales of Caring For Life's own produce, helped boost the Open Day's takings to over £16,000, an astonishing amount in that financial climate. Caring For Life also received an unexpected bonus in the form of a cheque and award presented by The Yorkshire Society as its charity of the year. The supermarket chain Asda, which has its headquarters in Leeds, offered help of a different kind, sending 16 volunteers to spend a day each month on the farm. It was their involvement that made it possible to rebuild so quickly the dry stone walls that had been demolished by vandals earlier in the year and no fewer than 80 of them came to assist in making the farm ready for Open Day.

Corporate sponsorship in the form of practical help by volunteer members of staff plays an important part in helping to maintain the Conservation Project and gardens and in undertaking new work, such as planting literally thousands of trees to create hedgerows to encourage wildlife and landscape the new road. These are tasks that are too labour-intensive for the staff to tackle but the charity is blessed with a devoted band of volunteers. More than 50 individual Christian supporters provide a vital service by committing to help out on the various projects on a regular weekly basis, freeing up staff for other duties and also enabling the charity to reach out to more people in need of its help. Even more important are the TFJs, the young people who give a whole year of their lives, usually after finishing university, for what is known as Time For Jesus. They work extremely hard, doing everything from sorting harvest offerings to cleaning toilets, and also, in a useful foretaste of a potential career in social work, standing in whenever additional staff are needed and helping out on the therapeutic projects and in the homes. Abigail, who attended the daytime activities, was singing the praises of one of the TFJs she had got to know during lunchtimes at the centre, enthusing about how great she was, how she multi-tasked and did so many things to help people. When the pastoral director agreed, saying 'Yes, that's right, all our Time For Jesus volunteers work extremely hard, helping others,' Abigail responded quick as a flash, 'It's a wonder they have any time for Jesus at all!'

Abigail may not have understood the concept of Time For Jesus but a growing number of those in the charity's care were responding to the love they had experienced by seeking to find out what lay behind it. The fortnightly Bible study group, held after hours for anyone interested and able to come, had 24 regular attendees. Meeting in the new music and drama room, they shared songs of praise, prayed together and began to explore what a Christian is, what church is all about and what it really means to follow Jesus. These were, and are, very special times which have been rewarded with a number of conversions.

Despite their many personal problems, the simple faith of these young Christians is deeply moving and demonstrates how spiritual understanding is a matter of the heart rather than the intellect. When discussing the nature of prayer and how it works, for example, Anna responded to the question 'What things does prayer change?' with the remarkably profound 'Prayer changes us, and how we see things!' Sometimes they ask challenging questions. When Benjamin, who had taken over 20 years to come to faith, told Esther that he had now become a Christian and that they would therefore be together for ever, he added 'Will there be photocopiers in heaven?' 'I really don't know', she replied, to which his answer was, 'Well, if there are, can I do your photocopying for you in heaven?' Even those who do not come to faith – and no one is ever under the slightest pressure to feel that this is expected – feel the benefit of these informal meetings. 'Caring For Life's Bible study groups have helped me in many ways', one very damaged young man reported. 'They have helped me to socialise with a range of people of all ages and from many different backgrounds which, in turn, has helped me to learn about, and understand, other people's views of both God and the Christian faith.'

That sharing the love of Jesus really does change lives is seen time and again. Words like 'Thank you' and 'I'm sorry' become part of the vocabulary of those who have always been completely self-centred. People who have been unable to control their anger find peace in themselves and the quiet confidence to reach out to others. One young man who had grown up in foster care and an endless series of foster homes was so traumatised by his experience of failed relationships that he avoided meeting people whenever he could. Though he loved the time he spent with the animals on the Agricultural Project, he refused to enter the centre, preferring to stand outside in all weathers even when it meant he could not share in the mealtimes. Gradually, however, he was persuaded to come in, not just because of the efforts of the staff but by the exuberant friendliness of those whom they cared for, who repeatedly invited him to join them for a cup of tea and a game of cards.

Another young man, Daniel, came to live in Tindall House after his mother died, and left him living on his own and unable to cope. It was the other residents who rallied round to comfort him when he burst into tears at his first Sunday lunch, and later, when he became extremely distressed at the farm, it was Aaron who brought him tissues, made him a cup of coffee and told him, in words that resonate with all who have been touched by Caring For Life, 'You'll be alright now mate. You'll be OK. We'll look after you. You're not on your own now. You've got a new family now. This is your family for ever.'

4

Caring in a Broken World

At the beginning of 2010 Peter Parkinson offered a disturbing assessment of the state of national social care.

> In our view, the plight of the homeless is worse today than when we began 23 years ago. Help available to the profoundly vulnerable people to whom we minister, and who are daily referred to us, is less accessible than it has been, and in some cases non-existent. The number of profoundly vulnerable people for whom there is now no long-term support available, is increasing all the time. No political party appears to have any intention of addressing the plight of this enormous body of people. It has been left to many Christian organisations and charities to help such people, and many of them have had to reduce or eliminate their services, as government funding is withdrawn or redirected to other areas. This is a crisis which is about to hit us at Caring For Life.

The charity's contract for Supporting People funding was due to end on 1st March 2010 and with it the £323,000 of government money, administered by the local authority, which helped to finance the residential homes and the Being There team's work in the community. The standard review of Caring For Life's eligibility for the funding had recently been carried out but some of the questions were simply incomprehensible to those with learning difficulties. When asked 'Are you happy with the service?' (meaning Wendy Margaret Home), Chloe innocently replied, 'Is that a bus service or a train service or a church service you're talking about?' Another lady, supported by the Being There team, was referred to as 'a service-user' by her interviewer and indignantly responded 'I'm not a service-user. I'm Claudia! Everyone calls me Claudia at Caring For Life.'

The problem for Caring For Life was that practically none of those in its care qualified for life-long support and funding from Social Services yet they were unable to manage living independently without substantial, ongoing and probably life-long care. 'You should not take so many difficult people!' was the response of the officer conducting the review but, as Peter pointed out, that is exactly why Caring For Life exists.

We have always accepted those rejected by other agencies, those needing life-long support, the difficult people, the ones to whom others say "No!". Since Christ has said 'yes' to us, how in the world can we say "No" to those no one else loves or cares about, those for whom no one wants to accept a long-term responsibility. Isn't that exactly what being a Christian is all about? Saying "Yes" to the lost, the losers, the difficult, the rejected, the hopeless. Isn't that just what Jesus did? Touch the untouchable, reach the unreachable, love the unlovable? So our response must be "Yes" – "Yes!" Always "YES!"

Whatever the Supporting People reviewers might say, Caring For Life was determined not to compromise its three core values: that care must be offered for life; that those in

Tindall House and Wendy Margaret Home must attend the weekday therapeutic activities at the farm if they had no other employment or commitments elsewhere; and that staff must understand the requirement to share the love of Jesus with those in its care and be able to do so. All the indications were that the funding would be withdrawn, but once again, after many heartfelt prayers and some lobbying of local councillors by outraged supporters, the department agreed to renew the contracts but only for a limited period: two or three years in the case of the Being There Project and a year or less for the two residential homes.

This was a reprieve, but since it was likely to be short-lived, it was even more essential than ever to continue to find alternative and regular sources of income. Expanding the supporter base was critical: all sorts of well-intentioned people would support charitable causes but only Christians could be relied upon to support a charity so firmly anchored on its Christian faith. Individual supporters were challenged to find two new recruits and persuade them to give just a pound a week. These would be mere drops into an ocean but the ocean is made up of drops and together they could create a mighty sea sufficient to replace Supporting People funding when it came to an end. Caring For Life's wonderful champions set to work and within the space of a few short weeks had started 15 support groups across the country from Somerset to Angus.

At Crag House Farm, everyone was working towards the idea of generating as much income as possible and as well as possible. The PR team worked indefatigably to secure grants for the projects, keeping in touch with those trusts which had long supported the charity's work, but also finding and approaching potential new donors. A newly appointed farm manager, Chris Cole, brought a wealth of farming experience to the Agricultural Project, expanding the numbers of cattle and sheep to make the best use of the recently acquired land and the new PAM building; free range egg production was wonderfully supported by the gift of 750 new hens by a supporter in Suffolk who continues to help the charity in this way; the Equestrian Project and its leaders began the process of registering with Riding for the Disabled and put two of the shires to foal so that future carriage horses would be home-bred. The Woodwork, Art and Craft and Horticultural Projects were all busy creating saleable items for the farm shop, which, together with the Granary café, had contributed a spectacular £157,000 of gross income over the previous year. And on 29th April HRH The Countess of Wessex returned for the formal opening of the new meat processing room and refurbished egg grading room, a superb facility built and equipped to the highest industry standards by Dunbia Meats. Stevie Dobson, Northern Ireland's first Master Butcher, who runs Dunbia's Butchery Academy, had been a regular visitor for many years, demonstrating his skills on Open Days, but also working closely with the men on the project. Now, trained by him, they would be able to add their own contribution to the charity's income by producing a whole new range of fresh meats, sausages and burgers for the shop and café. The countess spent time, as always, with many of the people attending the various therapeutic activities and also hosted an evening reception for local dignitaries which provided a valuable opportunity to build bridges.

Increasing levels of violence against those looked after by Caring For Life were a matter of great concern at this time. A fiercely independent 82 year old who was being preyed upon and having his money stolen on a regular basis; a 25 year old with significant learning difficulties whose girlfriend took almost all his money from him each week and whose friends threatened to beat him up if he told anyone about it; a 19 year old girl being subjected to serious threats of violence by her former partner and his mother and, having also been raped on the streets nearby, was too terrified to leave her own home. There was also Deborah, a lady in her late forties, who had fled an extremely dangerous and violent partner, only to have him track her down, smash up her flat and inflict serious injuries on her. The police installed a metal grid on her door, a panic alarm and a safe room but she was still so petrified that she jumped out of her skin every time her name was spoken and did not dare go outside alone. It was a Caring For Life support worker who called to pick her up and took her out to get cash, go shopping and even to a drive-thru so that she could get a coffee and have a chat without leaving the safety of the car. These were just a few of the tragic stories of the 139 people whom the Being There team were now supporting, all the while conscious of a growing waiting-list, already consisting of six men and 19 women in desperate need, but without the resources to help them.

Balanced against this were the heartening stories of those for whom Caring For Life was able to make a real difference. Dinah had remained in touch after leaving the psychiatric unit where she had been placed the previous year, and finally decided that she wanted to return to Wendy Margaret Home; it was a joy to see how once again she blossomed as she re-joined the friends she had made before, attended the daily therapeutic projects and even chose to go to the Bible classes. 'I have become a Christian. I believe in God and Jesus' she said as she prepared for baptism. 'My life has started to get better. My family leave me alone now and that helps.' And Caring For Life had its first wedding! Adam, who had lived at Tindall House for 22 years, married Chloe, a resident of Wendy Margaret Home, after an engagement lasting several years. Their wedding blessing service took place in the music room at Crag House Farm and Reuben drove them in the Equestrian Project's horse-drawn gig to their reception in the centre. They moved into their new home together, a flat near enough for them both to continue to attend the daytime activities at the farm. They were each assigned a Caring For Life support worker, an absolute necessity given that both were vulnerable and had multiple needs. Filling in the housing support forms when Adam first moved to the flat a few months earlier had provided some hilarious moments. When asked who he would like as his emergency contact, Adam fell silent. 'What if you fall into a diabetic coma and need urgent treatment?' his support worker asked. 'Who would you want us to ring?' There was still no response. Trying a different tack, his support worker asked 'Well, should we ring Chloe, or your mum?', only to receive the matter-of-fact reply, 'An ambulance!'

A wheelchair-accessible minibus to bring people to the farm had long been on the charity's wish-list but was simply unaffordable. It therefore seemed providential when, in the summer of 2010, the ideal vehicle became available at a cost of £40,000. Even this was far beyond what Caring For Life could afford but then came a miraculous turn of events of the type that had happened so often before in the charity's history. The executive committee had come together to pray specifically for funds to buy the minibus. As they were praying, Peter's wife Judith knocked on the door, apologised for interrupting prayer time, and brought in an unsolicited and unexpected cheque from a generous donor who had instructed that it could be spent on whatever was most needed. The cheque was for £40,000! A trial run was arranged and the minibus was purchased, enabling those who were physically unable to get to the farm or could not do so safely on public transport, to be picked up from their homes, delivered to the farm and returned home again after a day of stimulating activity and friendship. To see a depressed and poorly person arrive then at the end of the day leave smiling and laughing is to witness how small a window of opportunity is all that is sometimes needed to transform broken lives.

A further miracle was bestowed that summer. Eleven months earlier, in September 2009, the driving force behind Caring For Life since its inception, Peter Parkinson, had been diagnosed with advanced prostate cancer and a scan showed had that it already spread into his bones. The only treatment available for him was a course of hormone injections which has proved to be effective in keeping the cancer under control. A further diagnosis, of diabetes, added to the frustration of physical illness impeding his ability to commit himself fully to a workload that would have defeated even a fit and healthy man. When Peter went to his hospital appointment in August 2010, however, his urologist was surprised and pleased to inform him that his PSA level had dropped from an extremely high to a remarkably low count. Although delighted with this news, and grateful for the treatment which had literally given him a new lease of life, Peter also recognised that the prayers of the Lord's people were without doubt a huge contributory factor in this remission. In the reassuring words of the apostle Paul, God had once again shown that he 'is able to do immeasurably more than all we ask or imagine.'[13]

Peter's illness had, however, focussed attention on the need for succession planning to secure Caring For Life's

---

[13] Ephesians:3.20–21: New International Version.

future. The expansion of the farm's facilities would be pointless if there was not an equal investment in people to carry forward the charity's aims. It had always been difficult to find Christian staff with a sense of calling to such a sensitive, difficult and often upsetting ministry. As many of these extraordinary people were having to bear the additional burden of struggling financially because of their recent pay-cut, it was therefore decided to reinstate their salaries in full. Four of that year's six TFJs would also become permanent members of staff. Two new trustees were brought onto the board, Jonathan Birnie from Dunbia Meats and Gayle Pennant, an educational psychologist who had frequently offered her services on a voluntary basis at the farm. Additionally, Peter's elder son Jonathan, who with his brother Tim had been involved in the charity's work since its foundation, handed over all his remaining farming responsibilities to Chris Cole and took on the support and management of the Being There team and the residential homes. Tim assumed the equally important role of business director.

If Supporting People funding was withdrawn, as expected, then the charity would need to find almost £27,000 extra a month just to maintain its present work. But there was another, even greater challenge ahead. In January 2011 Peter shared with supporters his vision for new residential homes. First, a much larger replacement for Tindall House to fulfil the changing needs of its current gentlemen as they aged, right up until the point where they needed full nursing care, and also to take in more residents, including married couples, who required extra support beyond that which could be provided in the community. Tindall House itself could then revert to its original purpose, for which it was much more suited, offering a home to 16 to 25 year olds.

The same pattern could then be repeated for the younger ladies of Wendy Margaret Home.

There could be no doubt that this was the right thing to do, but was it the right moment to launch such ambitious plans? Caring For Life was just about managing to ride out the global financial crisis at Crag House Farm but a new enterprise, Caring For Life USA California, launched less than two years previously, had not progressed as the executive committee had hoped. This was in a large measure due to the very serious and ultimately fatal illness of the key person, Mike Castle, a dear friend of Peter, a huge supporter of Caring For Life and a crucial charismatic figure in getting Caring For Life USA off the ground. Caring For Life had offered a model, guidance and expertise in setting up the charity, and helped to train its staff, but it was always intended that it should be funded entirely from within the USA. Although Jeremy, who headed the work, and Mike's two daughters Elizabeth and Wendy did their utmost to ensure success, without Mike's input, guidance and inspiration, and without the backing of a supporter base like that enjoyed by Caring For Life in the UK, it could not survive in that economic climate. However, generous gifts from some of Caring For Life's supporters in the USA are still received here in the UK.

Caring For Life had to concentrate all its energies on securing its own future. Supporters now provided more than 56% of the charity's income, grant-making trusts a further 10.5%. 'At Caring For Life we do not believe our call is to ask you to support us and just wait for your gifts to come in', Peter assured readers of the monthly bulletin. 'We are convinced it is our God-given responsibility to do everything we are able to try to raise the finances we need, in order to sustain and to expand our ministry here.' A trading arm had

The Caring For Life family tours the newly acquired land at Crag House Farm, and prays in each field for God's blessing.

HRH The Countess of Wessex, Patron, unveils the plaques for the new Adult Learning and Arts Centre and the People and Animals Meeting building.

Juliet Barker, author, presents Peter Parkinson with The Yorkshire Society's Charity of the Year Award in 2009.

Jonathan Parkinson with Stevie Dobson of Dunbia in the new Meat Room. Stevie was very much the inspiration for the project.

Caring for the Longhorn cattle in the People and Animals Meeting building.

Members of the Drama Project enjoy applause following their production of scenes from Shakespeare's *Twelfth Night*.

Driving Minnie!

Guests at the official opening of the Granary Restaurant.

Playing the part of Christian in a performance of *The Pilgrim's Progress*.

A glimpse into the Art Room. 'All people are different' and so we celebrate the fact that 'all drawings are different' too.

Christmas Day at Caring For Life.

A member of the Being There housing support team visits a lady in the home found for her.

Jonathan Parkinson, now CEO, with his father, Peter.

The new Horticulture Project area in the beautiful glasshouse at Crag House Farm.

Caring For Life at play: a scene from a Silly Sports Day!

One of the gentlemen who was 'brought safely home' to Caring For Life shares his testimony at the 30th Birthday Thanksgiving service in February 2017.

therefore been set up whose sole purpose was to raise money for the charity by marketing its own produce and high quality British and ethically sourced goods. Many of the daytime activities were attracting new funding by expanding and branching out into new areas of ministry. The Equestrian Project was now registered with Riding for the Disabled and, drawing on the expertise of a new staff member Graham Cooper, who had worked for HM The Queen for many years at the Royal Paddocks at Hampton Court, horses had been trained to offer riding or driving. A carriage had been adapted to provide wheelchair access and a special saddle acquired with interchangeable parts to ensure that every rider was held securely in place, whatever their particular difficulty or need. For those with limited mobility, it was especially thrilling to be able to travel through the countryside, riding or driving these beautiful intelligent animals which seem to sense their responsibility and, despite their size, react with gentleness. The wonderful bond that can develop between horses and those attending the project was nowhere better described than by Dorcas, a much-loved lady with multiple and severe disabilities, whose special favourite was Minnie:

Minnie is a Shire horse and she's beautiful! Minnie knows that I come every Friday, she knows my voice and she talks to me. My wheelchair goes on the carriage and I hold the reins and drive her. When I've been alone I know she knows all my feelings; she talks to me like she's telling me, 'Don't be afraid!' I love her. I asked Graham, 'Will horses go to heaven?' I hope there are horses in heaven.

The success of one particular project, however, eclipsed all others, at least in terms of contributing to Caring For Life's income. The little Granary café and farm shop was now regularly attracting more than 1,250 customers a month; its turnover had risen from £51,000 in its first year to £190,000 in its second and £480,000 in its third. All that held it back from contributing more was its limited number of table settings and tiny galley kitchen so the obvious solution was to move to bigger and better premises. Providentially, just the right building was available for development: the dilapidated seventeenth century barn next to the Granary which had long been unusable and had become an eyesore. With a powerful imagination it was just possible to see its potential and an architect was duly employed to draw up plans for its conversion.

Finding the money to go ahead with the work would be more difficult. At the beginning of August 2011 there was not enough in the charity's bank account even to pay the staff's salaries. Once again, however, God provided in the most extraordinary way: the very day that it was needed exactly the right sum was paid into the account in the form of a £13,000 legacy from a supporter. This was an unexpected blessing, but at the forefront of everyone's minds was the looming financial black hole caused by the ending of Supporting People funding for both the residential homes and the Being There Project. It had been confirmed that Caring For Life's contract would end in January 2012 and with it a stream of income worth £323,000 every year. To the astonishment of other local charities in a similar situation, which were planning to close all or part of their operations and already asking Caring For Life to take on the people who would be ejected from their housing and hostels, Caring For Life remained resolutely determined to continue and even expand its ministry. It embraced the opportunities to have greater independence to carry out its mission on its own terms and to be freed from the bureaucratic burden which came with some funding. Unlike other social care agencies, which were almost totally reliant on government funding, Caring For Life was convinced that the Lord would provide for his work. 'The most generous people in the world are Christians!', Peter told them, 'And there is a reason why! Freely have we received, so freely we give!'

As the charity approached the silver jubilee of its foundation, it was a tragic irony that the situation for vulnerable people looked set to be worse than it had been a quarter of a century earlier. It was incumbent upon Caring For Life to survive and to thrive, not just as a sacred duty to minister to their needs but as a public demonstration to a disbelieving and secular world that the living God was truly walking beside them. 'The world is watching; those in our care are watching', Esther observed. 'Please pray with us that the God who owns the cattle on a thousand hills will graciously meet all Caring For Life's needs, blessing the work of our hands, and enabling us to share the love of Jesus with a broken world.'

5

Meeting a World of Need

Christmas at Caring For Life is always a very special time. Everyone in the charity's care receives cards and gifts, including a seasonal hamper, much needed items of clothing and toys for children: these are often the only presents they will receive. Those with nowhere else to go and no one else to turn to are invited to share the warmth, love and laughter of a proper family celebration at Crag House Farm. Staff and volunteers collect them in time to attend a special Christmas morning service, then they are served a traditional Christmas lunch. For most of them, this will be the only proper meal they will have that day and they look forward with great excitement to turkey and all the trimmings. One gentleman in the charity's care confessed that the first time he had ever had a Christmas dinner was when he was 16 years old. He remembered it because it was also his first Christmas in prison. 'Until then, we just had beans on toast for Christmas dinner, like every other day!'

Served by staff and volunteers at beautifully decorated tables with named places for everyone, carefully chosen presents supplied by local churches and extra gifts of toiletries and chocolates from generous supporters, each individual is made to feel important and loved. One elderly gentleman always stands up and, wobbling precariously as he hangs on to his chair, delivers a little speech thanking all those who have given him such a wonderful day, because, without Caring For Life, he would have been completely alone. A young lady who had only recently managed to break away from years of horrendous physical, sexual and mental abuse, during which she had been repeatedly imprisoned, came to the farm for her first Christmas. Never having been allowed any money of her own, or to go out to choose her own clothes, she had just enjoyed her first shopping trip to buy clothes for herself and gifts of her own choice for relatives. Baby steps perhaps, but ones which, with the support of Caring For Life, would help to put her on the road to a new life. For others, however, Christmas Day is only a bleak reminder of all that they have lost. Another lady who, for a couple of years, had been to the farm for Christmas with her young daughters then had them taken away from her and put into care with no possibility of being returned to her. There was no question that this was the right decision for the two girls, whose safety was paramount, but it only reinforced the feelings of failure and hopelessness in a woman who had herself suffered extreme abuse in childhood, genuinely loved her children and had been determined to care for them, even though it turned out she was unable to do so properly. Coming back to the farm at Christmas on her own was difficult for her, but it provided an escape from the constant images of children and happy families on the television and she would be among friends who loved her.

The 28th February 2012 was the 25th anniversary of the foundation of Caring For Life. Despite the enforced absence of some of its leading figures, it was celebrated in the charity's usual joyous style with parties, fancy-dress and energetic games for all those belonging to its extended family. There were other reasons to celebrate too. A local Sainsbury's store offered to give to Caring For Life all the food that remained unsold and had to be disposed of each day, a terrific help towards catering for all those attending the daily farm activities. The charity's patron, HRH The Countess of Wessex, paid a visit, hosting receptions for dignitaries and representatives of grant-making bodies who were helping to get the new Granary off the ground, cutting a special anniversary cake and, as always, meeting many of the beneficiaries and even sharing lunch with them in the centre.

Among those to be introduced was Paul, a recent recruit to the Being There team, whose life had come full circle. Due to horrific and violent abuse he had been taken into the care system for the first 16 years of his life and had spent time in the children's home run by Esther. He was a vulnerable young man who had come back to ask for help when he found he could not cope with living alone in a bed-sit, and was among those who took up residence in the charity's first home and was therefore one of the reasons why Caring For Life had been founded. 'I am very happy to be working for Caring For Life and providing for others the support I used to receive from them', Paul said, 'God has literally been more gracious with me than I deserve; probably true of all of us! Thank God for Jesus!' Another of those first young men also returned 24 years after having been given a home by Caring For Life. Nicolas had soon moved into accommodation of his own and successfully held down a job for many years but his significant learning difficulties and his own determination to work hard and long hours eventually led to a breakdown. He became extremely poorly, unable to cope with daily life and acutely at risk but he had never lost touch with Caring For Life and always came to the farm at Christmas. Now he was taken up again by the Being There team, helped to get the medication and treatment he needed and found a place on the Agricultural Project, which he loved. Safe once more, his confidence and happiness returning and, in time, perhaps able to seek employment again, his story demonstrated perfectly the importance of offering care for life, not just for the two years required of government-funded bodies.

The stresses and strains on those working for the Being There Project were described by one of its new staff members.

My job on the Being There team has challenged me on every level, especially the getting to places, and working through the ever-changing benefits system!! I've laughed and cried, gone through every emotion there is in dealing with the lives of such desperate and needy folk; I have felt their pain and and frustrations, experienced their joys too, and have sometimes just hugged and cried with them at times when that's all I could do ... What a privilege to bring Jesus to them where they are, wherever they are, however dreadful their situation."

Facing the sheer enormity of the problems lying ahead, there are always two options. As Peter put it, we can either allow ourselves to be overwhelmed and do nothing, 'Or we can say, "The task is far too big for us, we cannot do everything, we cannot take on the problems of the whole world! – But our Jesus can! And with his help we will do something!"' What is more, no matter how small or flawed our offering, through his grace and power it can be transformed into something great and wondrous. Time and again, Caring For Life's ministry had been blessed in many and unexpected ways and now, in its silver jubilee year, it was to receive amazing affirmation that its work was pleasing to him who had inspired it.

The success of the little Granary café and farm shop had demonstrated that one of the best ways to replace the income from Supporting People would be to build up and expand the charity's social enterprises but the conversion of the semi-derelict seventeenth century barn into a new Granary was estimated to cost more than £1.7 million. A magnificent bequest from a supporter allowed the initial work to begin but there was still a major shortfall which threatened the viability of the whole project. Having explored all other means, the only option left appeared to be to seek a loan. Banks proved unwilling, so as a last resort, Peter and his son Tim went to see one of Caring For Life's long-term supporters, explained the circumstances and the dramatic impact the new building would have on the charity's finances, showed him their business plan and finally asked him if he might consider offering them the necessary loan. He went away to discuss it with his family and when he came back said, 'No, we can't give you a loan'. Tim sighed, having expected nothing else, and so was absolutely astounded when the supporter then added, 'But we'd like to give you the money!' Despite this being the largest gift in the charity's history – over a million pounds – the donor insisted, in true Christian fashion, that he should remain anonymous.

As if this were not evidence enough of God's grace, a fortnight later an amazingly generous American supporter, Green Circle Growers, offered to buy Caring For Life a 1000 metre square state of the art greenhouse to replace its old poly-tunnels. The timing could not have been better as this would transform the capabilities of the Horticultural Project, enabling it to provide a constant supply of fresh home-grown produce for the newly expanded Granary as well as open a garden centre selling edible and ornamental plants to the public. It would also provide a more suitable (and warmer!) year-round home for those attending the therapeutic activities and enable the numbers taking part in them to increase. The greenhouse was supplied from the Netherlands and came equipped with the most up-to-date technologies for automatic irrigation and temperature and humidity control. Four Dutch builders arrived on site in August and worked daily from 6.30am till 7pm to erect the huge glass palace which would now be the first building visitors arriving at Crag House Farm would see. The Dutch team, like so many of those individuals and companies who came to build or otherwise work on the farm, were deeply impressed by what they saw happening there every day and a new friendship was formed. As a result, they ended up not only building the greenhouse but also offered to supply orchids, including the delightful miniature versions which they were currently developing, free of charge for two years. This generosity meant that Caring For Life would receive all the income from selling them in its garden centre without incurring any of the substantial costs of growing and transporting them from Holland.

On 25th October 2012 the new Granary restaurant and farm shop was officially opened by Dr Ingrid Roscoe, Lord Lieutenant of West Yorkshire and a long-standing friend to Caring For Life. The transformation of the old barn was truly astonishing: it seemed to have doubled or trebled in size, was filled with natural light, and, with its high ceiling, exposed oak beams and peaceful atmosphere, had an appropriately cathedral-like quality. All the fittings were also of the same beautiful pale oak, including tables and chairs for 70 customers and all the shelving and units in the large area dedicated to the farm shop and delicatessen. Along one side, behind a glass wall, the kitchen staff could be seen making delicious food to order, beavering away in the sort of calm and purposeful way which is the antithesis of celebrity television kitchens and occasionally greeting familiar visitors with a cheery wave and smile. For two gentlemen in particular, the new facility opened up a whole new area of work. Both were proud graduates of Caring For Life's own catering academy and had occasionally helped out in the old café. Eli, who had been one of the first residents of the original Tindall House and now lived in his own flat (which he always insisted, with great dignity, was actually an 'apartment') now charmed customers into spending more than they might otherwise have done in the shop, carried their bags and boxes out to their cars for them and ran errands for staff. Ethan, the newest and youngest resident of Tindall House, became a kitchen porter and, secure and happy working among supportive friends, developed his talents as the resident comedian and practical joker.

Ethan's transformation was remarkable. His childhood had been bleak, growing up unloved by his parents and victimised by his family because of his learning difficulties. Escaping home as soon as he could, he had drifted for some years until eventually he ended up living in a hostel where he was attacked and stabbed by some of the other residents. Concerned about his vulnerability, Leeds City Council referred him to Caring For Life, which found him a flat and a place on the Agricultural Project. He loved coming to the farm so much that he would get up at the crack of dawn to cycle there and was always one of the first to arrive. When a place became available in Tindall House, enabling him to attend the therapeutic projects at the farm every weekday, he moved in and flourished. Completely uninterested in Christianity at first, his attitude began to change when he was present at the last Open Day held in the marquee: 'It was raining really hard, I mean so hard you could hardly hear anything. Felix kept pulling Peter's coat and was telling Peter to pray that the rain would stop. Peter did, and then, amazingly, like straight away, the rain stopped. It made me start to think about God.' Ethan began to attend Bible studies and occasionally attended church. In 2011 he had a serious bicycle accident, rupturing his spleen and spending six days in hospital: 'I was really worried that I would not live,' he confessed, 'but I really knew deep in my heart that Jesus was with me from that moment.' An enthusiastic performer in all the Drama Project's productions, his conversion was completed when he took the lead role in John Bunyan's *Pilgrim's Progress*: 'I acted Christian and I became a Christian!' he declared, adding, in his baptism testimonial, 'I want to be baptized to show you all that I want to live a new life in Jesus and I want to use the gifts that Jesus has given me here in this church.'

Ethan's baptism was one of many among staff and those for whom they cared during a year which had begun with such trepidation as the charity embarked on a new course without the prop of government funding. To see a young man come to Christ through its ministry was the greatest reward, but there were others which were important, humanly speaking, because they publicly recognised the quality of Caring For Life's work. Esther had received a Lifetime Achievement Award at the Sue Ryder Yorkshire Women of Achievement Awards the previous summer; now Caring For Life was given the Duke of York's Community Initiative Award for 2012; at the same ceremony, Peter was presented with the Outstanding Leadership Award. It was yet another occasion on which the most fitting comment came from the psalmist, whose words were now inscribed over the glass entrance to the new Granary: 'Not to us, Lord, not to us but to your name be the glory.'

The Granary and garden centre were vital to Caring For Life's future financial security but they raised a dilemma. Crag House Farm is tucked away in the midst of fields in the countryside on the outskirts of Leeds: it therefore provided a peaceful haven where deeply traumatised and vulnerable people felt safe to come and free to stay without feeling that they were being observed or might encounter strangers. Now, the general public were being invited into the social enterprises at the heart of the farm – and even encouraged to do so by large signs erected at the roadside entrance. To cater for the increased number of visitors, as well as ensure that the farm remained accessible to staff, volunteers and beneficiaries during winter months, the new road had been resurfaced with tarmac, thanks to a further gift from Dunbia Meats which also financed the necessary expansion of the car park. In planning all these changes much thought had been given to keeping the public away from those areas of the farm which were dedicated to the therapeutic activities. This had to be done discreetly and without detracting from people's enjoyment of their visit, so designated wheelchair-accessible pathways were created to enable customers of the Granary and garden centre to wander down through the Conservation Project and experience a foretaste of heaven among the peaceful woodland, orchards and ponds which teem with wildlife.

The beneficiaries attending the weekday projects were thus protected from unexpected interaction with visitors and able to continue their activities without interruption. This was especially important for those who were fearful of strangers, such as Gideon, a young man in long-term care who, when he first came to Caring For Life, had such a limited vocabulary, ('yep', 'nope' and 'dunno' being his only response to questions) that it was extremely difficult to get to know him or feel certain that he understood what was being said to him. As a result of serious learning difficulties, compounded by a complete lack of nurture in his early years, he was unable to read, write, count or identify colours and unaware of what day or time it was: he did not even know his own age or when it was his birthday. (He was, however, a dab hand on the drums!) Unable to communicate how he felt, or why, his usual response to any problem was literally to run away. Working as part of a team on the Agricultural Project gradually drew him out to the extent that, after a year, he was sufficiently confident to accept the further challenge of joining the Literacy and Numeracy Project at the farm, which is run entirely by volunteers. Despite having to start at the most basic level by learning to identify the shape and sound of letters, and concerns about his ability to work with a female tutor, he showed surprising determination and perseverance. His progress was very slow but in the process he learned to engage with others and, miraculously, he found his voice.

After 18 months on the project, he announced that he was 'writing' a puppet show to perform at the Christmas party. His tutor Collette wrote his story down for him and, with the help of the Art Project, he worked for many weeks to create papier-mâché hand-puppets of a dragon, a knight and a princess. He sought out other members of staff to help him prepare and perform his little play, which had a surprisingly poignant twist in the tail: the fierce dragon turned out to be lonely so the knight took him back to his castle where he became the security guard. As one of his delighted carers commented, his achievement could not be overstated: his new-found skills transformed his life. From being totally withdrawn and inarticulate, he began to build relationships, tell jokes, give an opinion, make suggestions

and even offer reasoned explanations. Although he still
sometimes gets his words wrong, he has an uncanny knack
of expressing what is actually true. His most famous comment has entered the annals of Caring For Life as the per-
fect strapline for all its projects where a simple task could
always be done far more quickly and easily without the
'helpful input' of those being cared for: having worked hard
on helping with the hay-making, he congratulated those on
his team with the immortal words, 'Many hands make more
work!'

Gideon's story is a remarkable instance of God's grace
and blessing on those who strive to do his work on earth
but the frustration for all involved with Caring For Life is
that there is always so much more that can, and needs to,
be done. The workload became even heavier as the government began to implement a wholesale restructuring of the
welfare system in April 2013. This was a necessary reform
in the light of the ongoing financial crisis and Caring For
Life had always recognised the need to ensure that benefits
were received by those who genuinely needed them. It had
never supported those who were simply seeking to defraud
the system. As part of its commitment to the people in its
care, it had always tried to help them spend their time con-
structively and prepare them to enter the workplace if they
were able to do so: even a short time on one of the therapeutic projects can sometimes sufficiently rebuild the confidence of someone who has suffered a crisis to enable them
to move on and return to employment, knowing, of course,
that they have the safety net of returning should they want
or need to do so. The problem for Caring For Life was that
the majority of those in its care would never be able to do
this. They were both the most in need of welfare benefits
and the least able to help themselves obtain them. How do

you fill in a form if you cannot read or write, let alone understand the questions you are being asked, or if you lack the ability to explain adequately what your needs are?

The changes to housing benefits meant that many of those who were on Jobseeker's Allowance, the lowest form of benefit, would have to pay £10 a week or more in extra rent and council tax if they wanted to stay in their homes. For those who could not afford to do so, the only option was to move into a smaller, cheaper property. Within a month of the changes coming into effect, one member of the Being There team alone had to move eight of the ladies in her care, but Leeds, like most other cities in the country, did not have anything like the number of suitable one-bedroomed homes available for those who wanted or needed to move. Elisabeth explained the impact this had on her. 'I can't afford the extra bedroom tax now my daughter has left home. I'm in debt and I can't pay what they're asking. We need to move to a smaller property, but there aren't any. What are we going to do? I keep crying and me and Isaac argue all the time. I hate my life.'

Another deeply troubling aspect of the new system was the pressure to submit claims for the new benefits through the internet. After one letter of notification, applicants were supposed to put in their claim online and all future communication would then be by email. Failure to respond to the letter or to apply online before the deadline would mean an immediate stopping of all benefits. The vast majority of those looked after by the Being There team had no computers, email addresses or, indeed, the knowledge and competency to use them. Caring For Life was therefore inundated with requests for help, including from former beneficiaries who had been managing on their own but were now distraught and scared at the prospect of losing their benefits and homes. Stigmatisation by the press as 'skivers' and 'a drain on society' added to their anxiety and a number of these emotionally fragile people threatened suicide: one or two actually did attempt to kill themselves. Some with learning difficulties or mental health problems risked losing their benefits altogether because their natural instinct was to hide their letters so they could forget about them; others simply lost them in the general disorder of their homes. Without Caring For Life's help, large numbers of hitherto settled people were in grave danger of becoming homeless again.

Even those who successfully applied for the new benefits would no longer be paid fortnightly but be paid a monthly lump sum, out of which they would now be responsible for paying their own rent to a landlord, instead of it being paid direct. For those who already struggled to manage within a two-week timescale because they did not understand budgeting or financial deadlines, this was a major hurdle which could not be overcome without additional help and support from the already over-stretched Being There team.

All this came at a very difficult time for Caring For Life. In common with many other charities, income from supporters had dropped as the financial crisis continued and people were faced with hard choices about which good cause most deserved their money. Added to this was the unfortunate impression, created by the splendid new buildings and carefully tended gardens at the farm, that Caring For Life must be financially secure and no longer needed the little many of its supporters were able to give. This was deeply worrying because, regular donations, no matter how small, had always provided over 50% of the charity's income and were vital to fund its day-to-day running costs. Faced with the prospect of having to make significant reductions in staff and even close some of the projects to make ends meet, Peter repeated his pleas to supporters to remember that all manner of people would support a worthy cause but only Christians would support a Christian charity and that every gift, no matter how small, would make a difference. The staff themselves were the first to respond, again taking a substantial cut in salary, and supporters similarly rallied round, with unexpected legacies also helping to turn a very dangerous corner. 'I do believe that the Lord waited until we ourselves at Caring For Life, until my staff team were themselves giving, and giving sacrificially, before he began to open the windows of heaven to bless us', Peter acknowledged. 'I firmly believed that we could not ask the Lord to bless and honour us unless we as a staff team were ready to take our call to self-sacrifice seriously. It is a privilege to be a part of this ministry. If any member of staff fails to grasp this they should not be here. But it is a huge privilege to be supported by generous and often sacrificial people such as you, our prayer supporters. To you I say a very, very sincere thank you.'

6

One Life at a Time

Jacob was referred to Caring For Life from an emergency hostel which was greatly concerned about him and thought he needed long-term support because of his inability to settle anywhere. It was only after months of being looked after that he finally felt safe enough to explain why: for many years he had been a modern-day slave. Like others in the same plight, he had been taken from outside hostels or benefits offices with the promise of a wage and accommodation but then savagely beaten, forced to work punishingly hard for little or nothing, and threatened with violence and even death if he attempted to leave. The one time he did manage to escape, he was tracked down, abducted and forced back into servitude, leaving him now in constant terror of being found again. Supported by the Being There team in a new flat – his first home since leaving the care system – and taking part in the daily projects on the farm, he settled quickly and gratefully into the Caring For Life family, became engaged to a fellow beneficiary and began to attend church and Bible studies with her.

The Bible study groups were a constant source of inspiration as such badly damaged people, often with little intellectual capacity, eagerly sought to understand fundamental spiritual issues and apply them to their own lives. Anna, one of the first residents of Wendy Margaret Home, had changed since her conversion from being extremely aggressive and often out of control into a kind and joyful young lady with a real knowledge and understanding of the Bible. After one study session, at which she had been praised for her thoughtful answers, Anna asked Peter if he would wear her brightly coloured hair-extensions if she asked him to and he foolishly replied 'Anna, I will do anything for you!' Next morning she turned up with a beaming smile and the hair-extensions in her hand. With them was a carefully written note, with a smiley face, quoting Matthew: 5: 3: 'Let your "yes" be "yes", and your "no", "no"'! Of course Peter had to keep his promise. Not everyone was as well-versed as Anna. A discussion about Jesus's enemies prompted one gentleman to say 'One of them was that King Arthur, wasn't it?' 'No, not King Arthur!' Peter replied, whereupon he tried again: 'Oh yes, I remember, not Arthur, it was King Harold!' Esther gently suggested that perhaps he was thinking of King Herod.

Even those with no interest in the Christian ethos of Caring For Life become more empathetic towards others. Trying to explain in simple terms to one young man on the Agricultural Project who had severe learning difficulties that a cow which had given birth to a still-born had been given another calf to 'foster', prompted immediate concern for the adopted calf: 'Will he have to go back?' was the first question asked by someone whose own experience of fostering had meant being unwanted and abandoned. Another beneficiary showed his concern for a needy neighbour who had been on a drugs bender for four days and eaten nothing during that time by bringing him to the farm for breakfast. His guest was completely unknown to Caring For Life and should not have been there, but he was provided with a hearty breakfast and a volunteer sat with him to chat and find out what could be done to help him. While they were talking, Gideon came up and anxiously asked the volunteer,

'You'll stay with him, won't you? You won't leave him on his own? Someone will be with him all the time that he's here, won't they?' That Gideon should have been able to put himself in the young man's shoes was in itself surprising, but the fact that he had plucked up the courage to approach a newcomer to express his concern was amazing, given how long it had taken him to feel comfortable enough to speak at all, even to those he knew well.

Caring for people in the community was becoming increasingly difficult because of the lack of available local authority housing of any kind, let alone the one-bedroom flats which were, and are, most in demand. The Being There team work tirelessly to move desperately vulnerable people out of hostels and unsafe areas into suitable homes but sometimes the only option is private rented accommodation. Unfortunately, many landlords who accept tenants on benefits have property which is in the most deprived parts of the city where the risk of being preyed upon, intimidated and abused is particularly high. Looking through a list of available housing in May 2014, Esther was struck and saddened to see that it contained just one single bedroom flat. Not only was it in an area that was totally unsafe for the majority of Caring For Life's beneficiaries but the landlord had specifically stated that he would not accept anyone who was under 35 or who had risk issues. That effectively excluded most of those in the charity's care.

'We so desperately need safe housing of our own,' Esther pleaded, to which Peter added, 'Conscience demands that we do something to help.' Three years earlier Peter had sketched out his vision of a Caring For Life community, which would provide a life-long home for all those currently in its care, whatever their age or level of disability, and also offering homes for those most in need who were being supported by the Being There team: people like Dorcas and James, a gentle Christian couple, devoted to each other, who struggled to cope with Dorcas's increasingly poor health. Confined to a wheelchair from an early age, Dorcas had to be fed all her food and drink but also needed help to get up and go to bed, bathe, dress and undress; James had his own difficulties, having gone blind in his mid-twenties. Although their flat was adapted to enable Dorcas to get out into the garden she was unable to use the kitchen as the door was not wide enough to take her wheelchair. Dorcas was reluctant to move into more suitable accommodation because she did not want to move far from Crag House Farm which meant so much to her. Caring For Life volunteers would therefore visit them every week, taking frozen meals specially prepared for them in the centre kitchen, helping with their shopping and just taking time to sit, chat and listen. Until she became too poorly to do so, Dorcas would attend the therapeutic activities at the farm, including her beloved Equestrian Project. Though she had delighted in Peter's fulfilment of his promise many years earlier to provide her with 'a day-care centre', she would not live to enjoy the beautiful Christian home, suffused with the love and peace of God, which he envisaged. She fell asleep in Jesus in December 2014, with James and Esther by her side, and her ashes were buried in the sensory gardens at Crag House Farm, a place she had loved and a fitting resting-place for her mortal remains. One of the last things she said was 'Look after James for me' and that precious charge continues to be observed to the letter. James still receives his weekly visits but has also been taken into the Caring For Life family, joining the percussion group and choir and the Computer and Media Project where, thanks to a special piece of software, he is able to work on the computer and enjoy the company and banter of the office.

In her pastoral report to supporters on Open Day in June 2014, Esther was able to announce that more than 30 new people were now attending the daytime activities at the farm. This was mainly due to the expansion of the Horticultural Project made possible by the new greenhouse which had been formally opened by The Countess of Wessex the previous October. Presenting his report at the same Open Day, Tim Parkinson pointed out the scale of the financial commitment involved in providing 96 members of staff to work on three sites (the farm and the two residential homes) which all had to be maintain and on 17 therapeutic projects which needed to take in more people. Highlighting what a previous accountant had aptly dubbed 'accounting by faith', Tim admitted that nearly every month he wondered if there would be enough in the bank account to pay salaries and other commitments. Individual supporters now provided 55.5% of total income, with a further 8.04% and 8.22% coming from churches and charitable trusts respectively. Urging all supporters to go out and find just one more person who could donate a pound a week, he added that without their prayers and faithful giving, 'this little place on the outskirts of Leeds would not survive'.

The charity needed not just to survive but to expand in the face of a growing call on its ministry and long-planned changes at the helm now took place to facilitate this. Failing health had obliged David Kingdon to resign as Chairman of the Trustees, a post he had held long and faithfully since 1999. Bill Bygroves, pastor of Bridge Chapel in Liverpool and an old friend to Caring For Life, now took over, bringing his extraordinary spiritual gifts and leadership, enthusiasm and vision to the role. Peter's wife Judith stepped down as Secretary to the Trustees, having served in that role since the charity first started, and Pam Young was appointed in her stead. Gayle Pennant, whose skills as an educational psychologist had proved invaluable in developing appropriate care for those with learning difficulties or mental health issues, would now become pastoral director. Finally, in the biggest change of all, Peter Parkinson himself handed over his role as chief executive to his son Jonathan. He had planned to do this on his seventieth birthday but, concerned about his deteriorating health, the charity's patron had encouraged him to do so earlier. Peter's increasingly poor health in recent years had forced him to step back from many aspects of active administration, enabling Jonathan to acquire a wealth of experience to add to his amazing heart for Jesus. He would be ably assisted by his equally gifted brother Tim who became the new executive director. 'Both these appointments are timely and right', the charity's patron declared in a letter to supporters, 'and I fully endorse them'. The Parkinson family had always been at the heart of the greater Caring For Life family but it was Peter's truly inspirational – and forceful – leadership over more than 27 years that had transformed a handful of volunteers responding to a local need into a fully fledged organisation supporting a powerful ministry to the poor and vulnerable. Although he would no longer be involved in the day-to-day running, he had lost none of his commitment or drive and would remain closely involved, but focussing his attention on making his vision of Caring For Life accommodation into a reality.

There would be no alteration or diminution in the work of the charity or the way it looked after those in its care. More than 180 people were now being supported to live in the community. Each time someone was helped to move into new accommodation the Being There team would swing into action, cleaning, redecorating and refurnishing neglected homes, sorting out benefits, connecting utilities, paying bills and registering with local doctors. Many of these isolated people would be brought to the farm over the summer to take part in fun days which ranged from Highland Games and Silly Sports to a very popular Hollywood Day complete with award ceremony and Oscars for outstanding performance. The Being There team also organised a whole series of special days out, tailored to the particular needs of each group, such as those with mobility problems or young families. Supported by staff and volunteers, they would travel by car or minibus to spend a day at the seaside, making sandcastles, taking boat-trips and paddling in the sea, with a fish and chip supper before they were taken home again. For most of them this would be the only holiday they would have but, however brief, it would provide them with a fund of happy memories to tide them over the coming months.

The approach of winter makes life especially hard for those living out in the community. Darker mornings and evenings further isolate those who are afraid to leave their homes and those who do stay in are often so cold that they retreat to bed all day, unwilling to switch on even the heater supplied by Caring For Life because they are fearful of the cost. Christmas is dreaded as it will bring pressure to buy presents they can't afford, sometimes for relations they never see; families will incur debts they cannot repay because they have cancelled standing orders or taken out loans to provide gifts for their children; some will have no one to buy for, or who will buy for them. For those whose Christmas will be very different it is utterly heart-breaking to see a young man at one of the parties on the farm, excitedly clutching three small packages from Caring For Life supporters and telling everyone who will listen, 'I can't believe I've got all these presents! Thank you!'

Released from the confines of the four walls which cut them off from ordinary social contact, many of those who are cared for open up while on holiday or at the farm. 'They don't judge you here' and 'I wish I could come here every day' are phrases that are often overheard in their conversations. Many claim that Caring For Life has quite simply saved their lives. One Iranian gentleman who had escaped to the UK after being imprisoned and tortured for his Christian faith had to sleep on the floor of his lounge and use his kitchen as a bathroom because his injuries made it impossible for him to go upstairs. The Being There team provided him with food parcels, put money in his electric meter to allow him to heat his room and arranged for a medical assessment so that he could be rehoused. The Christmas dinner at the farm was his opportunity to thank them publicly, insisting that he would not be alive without the support he had received. Jeremy who had been cruelly rejected by his family, after spending some time in a hostel for the homeless, now lived in a high-rise flat where his habit of hoarding presented a danger to him and threatened his tenancy. Even though he would only occasionally feel emotionally strong enough to allow the Being There team to help with clearing surfaces and cleaning, he appreciated their commitment and the unconditional love they showed him, saying that he would have killed himself without their support.

'We try to see people as our Saviour sees them,' Jonathan declared at Supporters' Day in 2015. 'Individuals made in God's image; not problems but people; not heavy burdens, but brothers and sisters.' Luke regularly said that Caring For Life had turned his life around: one of four siblings taken into care because of their parents' chaotic lifestyle, he also had a serious degenerative condition affecting both his physical and mental abilities. When first referred to the charity he had a broken hip, the result of an electric shock caused by poor maintenance of his rented accommodation, and he was living with a so-called friend who abused and controlled him. Caring For Life moved him into an emergency hostel, where he was unfortunately again taken advantage of financially by other residents, and then, in an answer to prayer, a bungalow adapted for his mobility needs came available in a quiet and safe area. Luke was overjoyed to have his own home at last but it was the dignity and love with which he had been treated for which he was most grateful. 'At Caring For Life they've looked past the crutches and everything, and you're a human being. That's the greatest thing ever!'

The people who most need dignity and love do not always receive it from other agencies. Mark had been made homeless at the age of 18 following a sudden breakdown in family relations which also left him facing a court case. 'Social Services were very little help,' Mark claimed 'My social worker spent most of her visits on her phone and trying to get rid of me. She also tried to get me to sign a "blank confession" (which I flatly refused).' Forced to sleep rough for six months, he was beaten up and robbed several times, before being introduced to two gentlemen 'who would change my life for ever. They were from a little charity called Caring For Life. We sat down in a little room and [they] did something amazing – they listened.' Much to his astonishment, they agreed to help him. 'And they still said they would help even after I told them I wasn't a Christian!!'

Mark's experience is one shared by many of the vulnerable people who come to Caring For Life. Having been shunted from one agency to another, they inevitably feel so hopeless and useless that they expect nothing better. As one young man said sadly to his Being There supporter, 'I don't know why you bother with me.' In the wake of the changes to the benefits system, many more bewildered and struggling people found themselves on the wrong side of faceless bureaucracy and sometimes uncaring agencies. One of the first residents of Tindall House, who had successfully lived in his own flat for many years, was deeply worried about the letters he had been receiving from the Department for Work and Pensions and afraid that he was going to lose the home of which he was so proud. Jonathan offered to set his mind at rest by calling in and looking through the letters, prompting the grateful response, 'I don't know how people cope without Caring For Life to help.'

He was not alone. One gentleman with memory loss had his benefits stopped but did not know why: he resorted to stealing food from the supermarket on the grounds that if he was arrested at least he would be fed. When the Being There team visited him for the first time they found him eating cat food because that was all he had left in his cupboards. He was immediately presented with a food parcel and arrangements made for all his letters to go to Crag House Farm to safeguard him. One letter, however, was wrongly delivered to his flat, he failed to pass it on to his support worker, missed his benefits appointment and instantly had all his money stopped again, including his housing benefit, which meant that he fell into rent arrears. The proposed requirement that under Universal Credit all monies would be paid monthly into bank accounts places enormous hurdles in the way of those dependent on welfare payments. Banks are reluctant to open accounts for those who have poor credit ratings – which is the common plight of those who lack numeracy and budgeting skills – and demand forms of personal identification, such as a passport and utilities bills, which many do not have. One gentleman on Jobseeker's Allowance was reduced to saving up the money he should have spent on food to buy a provisional driving licence so that he could use it as the ID required by the bank to open an account for him.

Perhaps saddest of all was the fiercely private and independent lady suffering from a degenerative disease who, when called for a review of her benefits, could not bring herself to admit to a stranger the deeply humiliating effects of her condition. As a result she was found fit for work and lost all her benefits, putting her at risk of losing her home. The only way to appeal against the decision was to acknowledge to herself, not to mention to the reviewer, exactly how her disabilities affected her. The spirits of this once proud and stubborn lady were utterly crushed by this cruelty, she sank into depression and became suicidal. Caring For Life could only support her by continuing to fight on her behalf, supplying her with food and other essentials, and offering her unconditional love: it could not restore her dignity.

Many of those called for a benefits review appointment would be so terrified that they could not face it alone and asked that a member of the Being There team should accompany them. This was absolutely necessary in the case of those unfortunate enough to be summoned for their meeting in York, some 45 miles away: it was simply impossible for those with serious disabilities or learning difficulties to find their way on their own from Leeds to York on public transport.

Amid all the trauma of the review process, there were occasional funny moments. One anxious gentleman became so dry-mouthed during his interview that the assessor offered him a glass of water and set it on her desk in front of him. At the precise moment when she asked him 'Are you ever clumsy?' he managed to knock the glass over, spilling water all over her desk and only narrowly missing her computer keyboard. As she reassured him that it was not a problem and mopped up with copious amounts of tissues, his Caring For Life support worker quietly said, 'Shall we make that a yes?' The assessor smiled and agreed.

The amount of support necessary to ensure that beneficiaries receive their correct level of benefits has become a huge burden, taking up a great deal of time and energy that could be better spent elsewhere. While some of the more basic work can be done by the Being There team, the complex cases and appeals have to be handled by more senior members of the pastoral care team. Esther now found herself acting as Caring For Life's corporate appointee, authorised by the Department for Work and Pensions, to help manage the financial affairs, including welfare benefits, of 20 people who were unable to do so themselves. Both she and Gayle devoted long hours to ensuring that the needs of those in their care, which they could not articulate for themselves, were appropriately represented on forms and in interviews. So many people were requesting help, however, that by October 2016 it became necessary to appoint a new member of staff as a benefits support worker tasked solely with that workload. This was crucial to help those in such desperate need but it was an additional drain on the charity's income which, as always, was already fully committed elsewhere.

As Caring For Life approached its thirtieth anniversary the problems facing those in its care seemed to be greater than ever before. Further proposed reforms to the welfare system meant that even more people were now at risk of becoming homeless. In April 2017 the automatic right to housing benefit for those aged under 21 would end: only those who could prove that they were 'vulnerable' would qualify but there was no definition of what 'vulnerable' meant, or how 'vulnerable' a person would have to be to receive the benefit. More seriously, in a move that also threatened the future of Caring For Life's own provision, the government proposed to remove what it called 'enhanced housing benefit' – which paid an additional amount on top of rent for providing support to the tenant – for those living in supported accommodation. The National Housing Federation estimated that 82,000 specialist homes were under threat of closure, which equated to just under half of all supported housing in England, and plans to open a further 2400 were now cancelled. Companies offering sheltered housing pointed out that they would have to evict vulnerable elderly tenants who were unable to pay their rent and had nowhere else to go. Caring For Life, which had already lost the Supporting People funding for Tindall House and Wendy Margaret Home, faced the prospect of losing at least a further £47,000 in annual income for a vital aspect of its ministry. And, unlike other organisations, it was, and remains, committed to the sacred promise of providing care for life.

Over the years the two homes had offered a safe haven for many deeply troubled young people. Most had never known a home of their own, having grown up in care, and most lacked even the basic skills necessary for living on their own. Some would only need a relatively short period of time before being able to move towards independent living with the support of the Being There team. Eve, for instance, had spent nine years in an abusive relationship, isolated from friends and family and only 'allowed' to see her Being There support worker. When, with her help, Eve eventually found the courage to leave after a particularly bad incident, she was taken straight to Wendy Margaret Home.

> The girls and staff welcomed me without question. Wendy Margaret Home was a super place for me. Without it I would have stayed where I was unsafe and scared. The next day I came to the farm. Caring For Life dealt with everything for me; involving the police, collecting my things – just everything. The practical help kept me safe but it was the emotional support that changed my life. Living at Wendy Margaret Home not only gave me a safe place – it gave me a home and a family. I was a stranger but I was accepted and became one of them immediately, and allowed to adjust in my own time.

Five years later, Eve said, she was in a totally different, happier place, living in her own home with the confidence and motivation she had previously lacked to enjoy it.

> I know that I will always have Caring For Life behind me supporting me whenever I need it. Living at Wendy Margaret Home I was given encouragement and independence, as well as a structured environment. I have many good memories and though I'm happy I have my own home, I will always be glad I had that time there.

Some of the residents of the two homes, however, would be there for life, since they would always need a level of love and practical support they could not get anywhere else. How for example, could someone like this lady in Wendy Margaret Home ever cope in the outside world? As she was helping to prepare dinner for the ladies one night, a member of staff asked her how they would know when the carrots would be ready. After five minutes of deep thought and concentration, she replied, 'Well, I suppose we could just ask them!'

7

Not Problems but People

Caring For Life celebrated its thirtieth birthday on 28th
February 2017 with a special service of thanksgiving to
which all supporters, staff, volunteers and beneficiaries were
invited. Ten years earlier, Peter had acknowledged that, 'As
a ministry, and as individuals, all of us at Caring For Life
must declare – "Hitherto hath the Lord helped us!"', and
this was just as true now. The charity had never acquired or
maintained financial reserves to draw on in a crisis because
all its resources were committed to looking after those in
its care. As a result, nearly every approaching month-end
throughout those 30 years had caused anxiety as to whether there would be enough money to pay the bills. Although
there had been dark days, the ministry had survived and
expanded exponentially. '[The Lord] has been faithful beyond all our expectations,' Jonathan told supporters.

> For 30 years he has walked with us. In fact he has gone
> before us and prepared the way for us to follow … As we
> begin our 31st year I can't see the need for this work di-
> minishing in any way, shape or form. When you are on
> the coalface, seeing the practical challenges just growing
> and growing, then seeing the emotional trauma in the
> lives of these people, you just want to do more.

And Caring For Life is doing more than ever before. At
Christmas 2016 a record 190 hampers were put together

and delivered to people supported in the community. In a new initiative, 40 of the hampers also contained a specially compiled folder called 'Simply Delicious – Tasty Food Parcel Recipes': written in simple English and with photographs of each stage of the recipe for those who struggled to read, it aimed to encourage those with limited cooking equipment and few, if any, store cupboard ingredients, to cook healthy and interesting meals for themselves and their families. In line with all the Being There's work, this was a practical response to a recognised need, helping to keep the most vulnerable from neglecting themselves and consequently falling into the ill-health and depression which ruins lives.

The Being There team is increasingly caring not just for isolated and vulnerable individuals but for families with small children: teaching parenting skills to those who have themselves suffered at the hands of their own parents, supporting single parents attending child protection meetings or custody hearings, and building family relationships and friendships by organising day trips, picnics and visits to the farm. This is work which will have a major impact not only on the families themselves, but also on future generations by helping to break the pernicious cycle of abuse which has trapped so many in desperately unhappy lives. The immediate effects are obvious: one gentleman who had been through the charity's programme recognised that his baby daughter was in danger of fatal abuse and, following the advice and training he had received in what to do in such circumstances, saved her life. It cannot be stressed enough how important this strand of Caring For Life's work is in helping to provide a long-term solution for the family problems that are so often the root cause of homelessness.

The weekday therapeutic projects on the farm have grown in number and in capacity, thanks to the acquisition of more land and the extraordinary new facilities built over the previous decade. There are now 17 different activities on offer, including the mechanics workshop which maintains and services all the farm vehicles as well as teaching repair, servicing and valeting skills useful for those capable of moving towards employment. Every project has expanded its intake and the quality of experience it offers. The Agricultural Project, for instance, has become a highly successful breeder of pedigree Lleyn sheep, allowing those involved, who have achieved so little success or recognition in their own lives, to share in the triumph of their flock winning awards at county shows and becoming Regional Breed Champions in 2016. More than a hundred different people now come to the farm every week, among them a set of 'glamorous ladies' who always dress up to the nines to attend the Art Project which is the highlight of their week. It is not just the beneficiaries themselves whose lives improve as they enjoy structured activity in beautiful surroundings, supported by staff with endless reserves of patience and unconditional love. As they become calmer, happier, more motivated and fulfilled, their families also reap the benefit, helping to spread the light of the love of Jesus a little further out into the darkness of troubled, dysfunctional lives.

The appointment of a benefits support worker has also been a life-changer for those in the charity's care. Most of those who come to the farm for the therapeutic projects have no social worker and cannot access advice or assistance elsewhere. Having someone who can read their letters, understand the application process, help them put into words their own particular needs and find them the appropriate benefits, is vital in helping to prevent deeply damaged people (whom the system is designed to support) from slipping through the net. And when the wrong level of benefits has been awarded, or the applicant's circumstances change, there is someone who cares about them and will help to guide them through the appeals process. Again, this is a practical example of sharing the love of Jesus which fundamentally affects every aspect of an individual's life and of those around them.

The opening up of Crag House Farm to social enterprises has expanded Caring For Life's ministry in unexpected ways. These include the new Granary restaurant overlooking the Conservation Project; the original Granary, now a coffee shop; the farm shop and delicatessen showcasing Caring For Life's home-grown meats, eggs, preserves and pressed apple juice while also championing other small suppliers, many of them local; the nursery in the new greenhouse with its wide range of plants for house and garden and items ranging from bird feeders to planters made on the Woodwork Project. All these ventures make a substantial contribution towards financing Caring For Life's work but they are also social enterprises with a heart, reaching out both to people who want a wonderful experience and quality products and to those who need to share a burden. The staff are there first and foremost to share the love of Jesus and many customers have responded gratefully, becoming regular visitors, and even supporters of Caring For Life.

Ten years earlier, the future of Caring For Life had seemed to be on a knife edge. The loss of Supporting People funding threatened to reduce, or possibly even end, the charity's ability to provide residential homes and support in the community. But, in the famous words of the Christian poet William Cowper, 'God moves in a mysterious way, His wonders to perform'. Re-energised by the need to replace the funding, and more determined than ever before to stand by the Christian principles upon which it was founded,

Caring For Life had moved forward in faith and the Lord had blessed its work in ways which could not have been foreseen. The prayers and sacrificial giving of its faithful supporters now provide a magnificent 63% of its annual income. Answerable only to them, and to the Master in whose footsteps they walk, the charity has been able to share the love of Jesus freely with those in its care and reaped the reward of seeing some of them become his disciples too.

But what of the future? The next 30 years? The charity now has a more secure and solid financial basis on which to build but it faces the same challenges: a world of need which seems only to increase and deepen. There has been an escalation in the amount of violence inflicted on those in its care, with predatory individuals and groups targeting them and forcing them to hand over their benefits, or into prostitution, or modern day slavery. With around a third of marriages ending in divorce and relationship breakdown commonplace, many more children are growing up in un-stable and dysfunctional homes and are at risk from their parents' new partners and siblings. As the safety net of state-sponsored social welfare shrinks, larger numbers than ever before of deeply damaged and vulnerable people are stranded without the means or ability to care for themselves. 'I recognise that we can't solve every problem and we can't do everything,' Jonathan told supporters, 'but with God's grace and, I pray, with your love and support, we shall be able to do more than we do now.'

Continuing to grow Caring For Life's self-financing and to increase its supporter base remain priorities for the future but it is also incumbent on the charity to fulfil its promise to care for life, not just for the short-term. The need to find a new home for the ageing residents of Tindall House be-comes increasingly desperate. The vision is to build a home within a home: each bedroom would have its own en-suite washroom and kitchenette to ensure complete privacy and, eventually, allow for nursing care. There would also be communal facilities, including a dining room, so that up to a dozen gentlemen could continue to enjoy the companionship which makes the current Tindall House truly a home. The search for suitable land and for a house to convert into two flats to provide safe accommodation for those at imminent risk is on-going: a building fund is in place, thanks to several legacies made for this purpose, but more money will be required if the vision is to become a reality – though not at the expense of supporters' regular giving which is crucial to uphold Caring For Life's wider ministry.

Just how much that ministry is valued by those it cares for is expressed time and again. 'Thank you for giving me a chance to shine!' said one gentleman, an enthusiastic participant in the Drama Project whose problems with short-term memory loss meant that he could never remember even the shortest of lines – and so brought the house down when, with supporters willing him on, he faultlessly performed the entire 'Once more unto the breach, dear friends!' speech from Shakespeare's *Henry V*. 'Caring For Life is my first love family,' said Ethan, going on to explain, 'My real family didn't care about me, didn't love me and left me. Caring For Life is my family, and the first family that has loved me.' A lady supported by the Being There team and asked to think of one thing for which she was thankful that day replied unprompted, 'I'm thankful for you, my dearest and only friend.' Nathan said, 'I was brought up on a bad estate and I was still in those bad ways when I was older. I always knew there was a different way and a different life, and I dreamed of my life being like that. That's what I've found now, here at the farm, that new way of life I dreamed of. Now I'm trying to help my grandkids find the right path in life.' He summed up how he felt about coming to the farm in just three words: 'lucky', 'privileged' and 'content'.

'Caring For Life means everything to me,' declared Hannah, who had suffered years of agoraphobia and lost main residency of her children as a result of being unable to take them to school or, indeed, anywhere else. Her life had gradually been transformed by the support of the Being There team, who gave her coping strategies, accompanied her to hospital for an emergency operation, persuaded her to attend the Art Project and then suggested she work in the farm shop where she rediscovered her sense of self-worth and a determination to fulfil her teenage dream of going to university. 'Caring For Life is the family you always wished you'd had', Hannah added. 'Unconditional love, non-judgmental, accepting, kind, loving and encouraging. I'd be lost without them. Can't thank them enough for giving me hope for the future and my life back again.' Perhaps the last word should go to Eve, who had been rescued from an abusive relationship and seen her life turned around by the support she had received.

I've said thank you many times to everyone at Caring For Life but have always been told it's not thanks they want, but the reward Caring For Life gets is the difference they've made in my life. And I think that says everything about Caring For Life and all the staff and volunteers who work tirelessly to make a difference. Caring For Life really does mean Caring For Life … Thank you.

There are so many more Ethans and Nathans, Hannahs and Eves out in the world; surviving not living; unloved and not expecting, or hoping for, love; waiting to be rescued and brought into the embrace of the Caring For Life family. As Christians it is our duty and, surely, our joy to do everything we can to support Caring For Life and to bring them safely home.

8

What Can I Do?

1. **Pray** – The work and ministry of Caring For Life has always been "covered" with prayer and the charity has been sustained and has grown thanks to the regular prayers of so many people:praying daily as individuals,praying weekly and monthly as churches and support groups. We need this to continue into the future. If you would like to keep up to date with things to pray for at Caring For Life, you can:

   a. visit our website for daily prayer points, which are given to and uploaded by beneficiaries who take part in our Design and Media Project
   b. pray in your church (contact us to let us know and we will be pleased to start sending our churches noticeboard prayer points, each month)

2. **Donate** –Remember that "drops into an ocean become an ocean of drops":

   Direct Debit – regular monthly donations are at the heart of the charity's income, both small and large. Details can be found on the charity's website www.caringforlife.co.uk.

One-Off Gifts
- PayPal via the charity's website www.caringfor-life.co.uk.
- Credit Card donation via phone - contact CFL's office 0113 230 3600
- Direct to bank - contact CFL's office 0113 2303600 for bank details
- Cheque payable to "Caring For Life" - post to: Crag House Farm, Otley Old Road, Cookridge, Leeds LS16 7NH

3. **Become a Supporter** – Sign up as an individual to receive the monthly prayer bulletin by post or email. (This contains daily matters for prayer, as well as stories from the projects and a message from the CEO.) To set this up, please contact us on 0113 230 3600 or send a request via the website email: info@ caringforlife.co.uk.

4. **Join one of our UK-wide support groups** – Contact CFL's office 0113 230 3600 to find out if there's one in your area. These groups meet quarterly to fundraise, to learn more about CFL and to pray.

5. **Leave a legacy** - Enabling men and women to find a safe home, a family and most of all, the love of Jesus. Legacy leaflets are available on request from CFL: 0113 230 3600; Crag House Farm, Otley Old Road, Cookridge, Leeds LS16 7NH.

6. **Fund-raise** – Here are just a few ideas: CFL's annual "Pause For A Cause" coffee mornings, strawberry cream teas, sponsored run/walk/silence.

7. **Contact us** on 0113 230 3600 / info@caringforlife. co.uk for promotional materials. Alternatively, you can download and print off the materials from our website (but don't forget to let us know what you plan to do, so we can help to advertise and promote it).

8. **Invite us to speak at your church** – We would be thrilled to come and share more about the charity and how the Lord is changing lives for the better. We will travel, and value the support that comes from all areas of Great Britain. Phone us on 0113 230 3600 to find out more.

9. **Get your company involved** – Volunteer team days at the farm, fund-raise as a staff team –e.g. have a cake bake at work,collect gifts for beneficiaries at Christmas, nominate CFL as the company's "Charity of the Year"

10. **Support the charity's social enterprises** –The Granary Restaurant, the Farm Shop, the Nurseries and Coffee Shop – all located at Crag House Farm, open Mon – Sat, 9am-5pm. ALL profits go to the work of the charity. (Visit www.craghousefarm.co.uk to find out more)

11. **Follow and share** –
    Facebook: @CaringForLifeCharity
    Instagram: @CFLCharity
    Twitter: cflcharity

For more information about any of the above, contact Caring For Life via the website www.caringforlife.co.uk, send an email to info@caringforlife.co.uk or get in touch with the charity's PR team on 0113 230 3600, at Caring For Life, Crag House Farm, Otley Old Road, Cookridge, Leeds LS16 7NH or via email to pr@caringforlife.co.uk.

Thank you!